UNIVERSITY OF ILLINOIS

UNIVERSITY RESEARCH BOARD

ELECTRONIC DIGITAL COMPUTER

ORDVAC MANUAL

October 31, 1951

Contract No. W11-022-ORD-11362
RAD ORDTB 9-10675
ORD Proj. TB3-00075
Negotiated Under ASPR 3-205

PREFACE

This manual describes a computing machine called ORDVAC
which has been constructed by the University of Illinois under
a contract from the Ordnance Department for the Ballistic Research
Laboratories of Aberdeen Proving Ground. The number of this contract is:

> Contract No. W11-022-ORD-11362
> RAD ORDTB 9-10675
> ORD Proj TB3-0007J
> Negotiated under ASPR 3-205

The contracting agency was the Chicago Ordnance District. The
period of the contract is April 15, 1949 - October 31, 1951.

The logical structure of ORDVAC is patterned after a
machine described in the June 28, 1946 report, "Preliminary Consideration of the Logical Design of an Electronic Computing Instrument" by Burks, Goldstine and von Neumann of the Institute for
Advanced Study. The University of Illinois received helpful information and suggestions arising from discussions with J. H.
Bigelow, H. H. Goldstine and J. H. Pomerene of the Institute for
Advanced Study, especially during the early period of construction
of the ORDVAC. In addition drawings pertaining to the arithmetic
unit and memory of the machine at the Institute for Advanced Study
were furnished to the University of Illinois and some parts of these
drawings, such as the registers, have been copied for ORDVAC.

While it was first planned to build ORDVAC from circuit drawings obtained from the Institute for Advanced Study, this intention was later changed and most of ORDVAC is constructed from circuits designed at the University of Illinois but using the fundamental flipflop, gating and cathode follower circuits originally used at the Institute for Advanced Study. The registers, complement gate and clear drivers were copied from the machine developed at the Institute for Advanced Study and the Teletype units are of the kind developed at the National Bureau of Standards for the Institute for Advanced Study. Except for these, responsibility for the design of ORDVAC rests with the University of Illinois.

    The University of Illinois has received the cooperation of members of the staff of the Ballistic Research Laboratories in the procurement of materials, and the assignment of members of the staff from Ballistic Research Laboratories during the final phases of the construction of ORDVAC. The staff members so assigned are: Dr. P. M. Kintner, Mr. G. H. Leichner and Mr. C. R. Williams. Dr. L. A. Delsasso and Dr. R. F. Clippinger of the Ballistic Research Laboratories have followed the work from its inception.

    Through arrangements made by Dean L. N. Ridenour, the University started the construction of ORDVAC about April 15, 1949. The construction of the machine has required the efforts of a number of individuals. Those who have been associated with the work during the major portion of the total period are:

iii

K. W. Bartlett	G. W. Michael
E. L. Hughes	J. P. Nash
W. E. Jones	J. E. Robertson
T. E. Kerkering	T. Shapin, Jr.
R. L. Liu	A. H. Taub
H. E. Lopeman	H. M. Walker
R. E. Meagher	J. M. Wier

An additional number of persons have aided the work during a part of the period. These persons are:

T. J. Bigelow	E. F. Moore
G. F Bland	Mrs. A. L. Searls
Mrs. Caroline Brown	M. D. Shapiro
J. P. Cedarholm	A. F. Spero
D. R. Clutterham	R. W. Tackett
Mrs. Helen T. Ernst	D. J. Wheeler
D. B. Gillies	D. G. Williams
Mrs. Natalie R. House	Mrs. Dorothy M. Wilk
R. T. Gregory	

The ORDVAC was provisionally accepted (pending delivery) by the Ballistic Research Laboratories on the basis of tests conducted between November 15, 1951 and November 25, 1951 at the University of Illinois. The machine was dismantled starting February 11, 1952 and shipped to the Ballistic Research Laboratories on February 16, 1952. On March 5 - 6, 1952 it successfully performed the three final acceptance tests consisting of: (a) the operation of the "final test" routine for twenty hours with one error, (b) the operation of a memory "read-around" test routine requiring that the memory could be consulted 10 times at each of its addresses without causing a failure at any other address; this was repeated five times, and (c) the operation of a memory flaw test for 30 minutes without an indication of a failure. The ORDVAC was moved to the Ballistic Research Laboratories under contract:

DA-11-022-ORD-680
SUB-RAD 52-56
ORDTB 2-1002
Project TB3-0007

The work in the University has been administered chiefly by an executive committee of the Computer Sub-committee of the University Research Board. This committee has consisted of: Professor N. M. Newmark, Chairman, Professor A. H. Taub, Vice-Chairman, Professor R. E. Meagher and Professor J. P. Nash.

ORDVAC CHARACTERISTICS

Machine Type	Parallel, Asynchronous
Register Capacity	40 Binary Digits
Memory Capacity	1024 Words of 40 Binary Digits
Adder Carry Time	9 1/2 Microseconds
Allowed Carry Time	13 "
Addition Time	44 "
Multiplication Time (all ones, positive multiplier)	1040 "
Multiplication Time (all zeros, positive multiplier)	610 "
Division Time	1040 "
Memory Period	24 "
Time to Load Entire Memory	38 Minutes
Time to Print Contents of Entire Memory	38 Minutes
Number of Tubes	2718
Machine DC Power	8.3 K W
Machine AC Power	8.8 K W
Total Primary Power (Including Power Supplies and Blowers)	35 K W
Kind of Input	5 Hole Teletype Tape
Input System (Space is 5 holes)	Sexadecimal
Output System	Sexadecimal Teletype
Number of Digits Assigned to an Order	9
Number of Digits Assigned to Memory Address	10
Number of Orders Available	Greater than 50

NOTE: Time measurements are to $\pm$ 5%. Arithmetic operation times do not include time for obtaining operands or orders from the memory.

Front View of ORDVAC

Rear View of ORDVAC

Front View of ORDVAC Without Covers

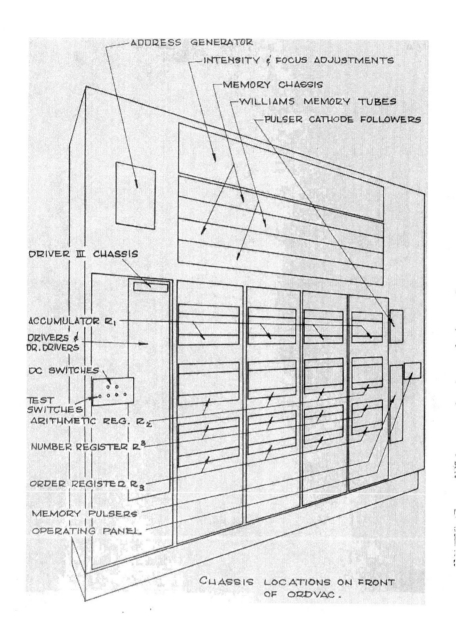

ADDRESS GENERATOR
INTENSITY & FOCUS ADJUSTMENTS
MEMORY CHASSIS
WILLIAMS MEMORY TUBES
PULSER CATHODE FOLLOWERS

DRIVER III CHASSIS

ACCUMULATOR R_1
DRIVERS &
DR. DRIVERS

DC SWITCHES

TEST
SWITCHES
ARITHMETIC REG. R_2

NUMBER REGISTER R^3

ORDER REGISTER R_3

MEMORY PULSERS
OPERATING PANEL

CHASSIS LOCATIONS ON FRONT
OF ORDVAC.

x

Rear View of ORDVAC Without Covers

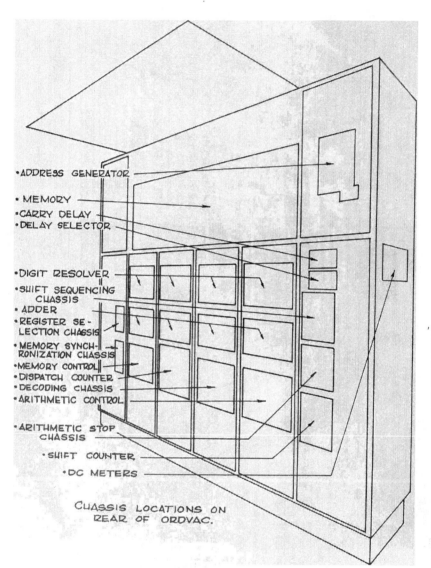

- ADDRESS GENERATOR
- MEMORY
- CARRY DELAY
- DELAY SELECTOR

- DIGIT RESOLVER
- SHIFT SEQUENCING CHASSIS
- ADDER
- REGISTER SELECTION CHASSIS
- MEMORY SYNCHRONIZATION CHASSIS
- MEMORY CONTROL
- DISPATCH COUNTER
- DECODING CHASSIS
- ARITHMETIC CONTROL

- ARITHMETIC STOP CHASSIS

- SHIFT COUNTER
- DC METERS

CHASSIS LOCATIONS ON
REAR OF ORDVAC.

xii

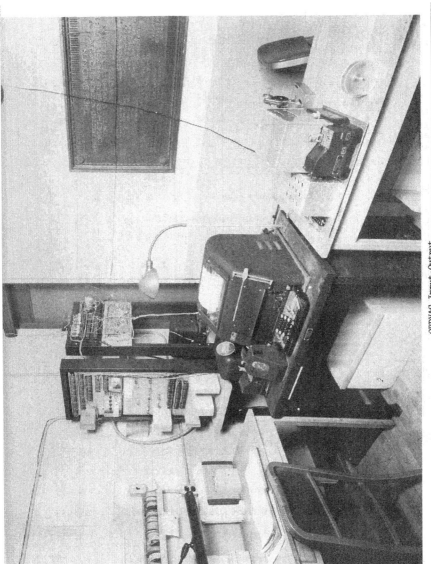

ORDVAC Trnsmt.-Orit.mt.

CONTENTS

CHAPTER 1

GENERAL DESCRIPTION OF ORDVAC

The purpose of this chapter is to give a brief description
of the various parts of the electronic digital computer called
ORDVAC and to discuss the over-all organization of this machine.
Since various parts of the machine use different representations
of quantities with which the machine deals, it will be necessary
to review briefly the "languages" employed by ORDVAC and the methods
existing in the machine for dealing with these languages.

1.1 INTRODUCTORY REMARKS. ORDVAC is a general purpose
computer capable of carrying out individual arithmetic operations
at high speed. If this machine were to be used as a desk calculator
where each individual operation would be selected by hand and if the
numbers to be operated on were also provided to the machine by hand,
the time saved in carrying out the arithmetic operations would not
materially reduce the time of a complete calculation involving a large
number of operations. The reason for this is that the time required
for arithmetic operations is usually only a small fraction of the time
required to carry out a mathematical computation. A machine which
is to do computations rapidly must therefore be designed in such a way
that it can do automatically those operations which a human operator
with a desk calculator must do with his fingers or with paper and
pencil. This has been accomplished in part in the ORDVAC by providing

1

it with an aggregate of 40 cathode ray tubes and 800 vacuum tubes called the memory.

In order to use ORDVAC effectively in any computation its memory must be fully or partially filled before the problem begins. This is accomplished by the part of the machine called the input. It uses teletype tape previously prepared by an operator using tape preparation equipment. However, ORDVAC is capable of controlling the operation of its input in that it can determine when to read information from the tape. The present input to ORDVAC is capable of filling the entire memory in 38 minutes.

ORDVAC is capable of printing out information from its memory. The equipment used for this purpose is called the output and includes two teletypewriters. Teletype tape may also be punched by ORDVAC if it is desirable to have the output on tape. The equipment used for output is in some part the same as that used for the input and it is convenient for the purposes of this discussion to refer to the equipment mentioned in this and the preceding paragraph as the input-output equipment.

The part of ORDVAC capable of carrying out arithmetic operations on numbers supplied to it is called the arithemtic unit. It consists of about 1100 vacuum tubes and is subdivided into the following units whose functions will be described in Section 1.3: Two double shifting registers R_I, and R_{II}, a register R^3, complement gates, an adder, a digit resolver and clear drivers.

2

ORDVAC is a parallel machine. That is, most operations performed on a set of digits which may represent a number or all or part of an instruction to the machine are performed simultaneously on all the digits. For example, when a 40 digit number is transferred from the memory into a register of the arithmetic unit, all digits are transferred simultaneously. Similarly when a number in R^3 is added to a number in the accumulator, the steps in this process are carried out on all the digits at the same time.

The remaining electronic circuits in ORDVAC, consisting of about 500 tubes, constitute the control. These circuits are primarily combinations of four kinds of logical elements:

1. The flipflop,

2. The "and" circuit,

3. The "or" circuit,

4. The "not" circuit.

The flipflop is a device which can indicate one or the other of two states and which can be changed from one state to the other. The two states can be indicated in any of a number of different ways such as, for example, "plus" or "minus", "yes" or "no", "on" or "off". In the ORDVAC the names given to these states are "zero" and "one".

The other three logical elements perform functions which are quite well described by their names. The "and" circuit has two inputs and one output which will have a signal on it if, and only if, there is a signal on each of the inputs. The "or" circuit is similar except that there will be a signal on the output if there is a signal on either one or the other of the two inputs.   The "not" circuit has a signal on its output if there is no signal on the input and no signal on the output if there is a signal on the input.

The _state_ of the machine at any time may be defined by the state of the flipflops in the machine. It is the function of the control to determine the state of ORDVAC and to change this state in accordance with the instructions provided to ORDVAC via the input and the memory.

1.2 NUMBER SYSTEMS USED BY ORDVAC.   ORDVAC uses several number systems. The basic one is the binary or base-two system. This system is convenient because it requires only the two digits 0 and 1 for number representation and therefore flipflops or any other two-state devices can be used. Moreover, the logical structure of the machine is based upon a two-state logic (where all decisions are of the yes - no type), so that an over-all consistency is obtained. Many operational economies can be realized with a binary system, and the disadvantages inherent in an unfamiliar system can be overcome by requiring the machine to make all of the necessary conversions to and from the decimal system.   The ORDVAC arithmetic unit has a fixed point number system and handles numbers in the range -1 to 1. ORDVAC can be programmed for any number system. The fixed point system requires a simpler control.   Numbers must be scaled to stay within range.

The choice of the range -1 to +1 is dictated by the fact that the product of two numbers in this range is likewise in range. The manner of handling negative numbers is chosen because of the simplicity of addition and subtraction. These operations are discussed fully in later sections.

Binary Numbers. In normal operation ORDVAC uses a representation in which numbers are represented by 40 binary digits. The leftmost digit is a sign digit and the other 39 digits are genuine binary digits, with the binary point immediately to the right of the sign digit. However, the arithmetic unit treats the first digit (the sign digit) as an ordinary binary digit. This means that the machine will represent numbers by using the range from 0 to 2, and we shall see that we then have numbers in the range $0 \le x < 1$ represented by numbers in that same range while numbers in the range $-1 \le x < 0$ are represented by numbers in the range $1 \le \bar{x} < 2$.

The usual nomenclature is to refer to the leftmost (or sign) digit as 2^0, the next as 2^{-1}, and the rightmost (or least significant) digit as 2^{-39}. For numbers between 0 and 1 the machine representation is correct if zero in the sign digit represents a plus sign. Thus

$$a_0 . \ a_1 \ a_2 \cdots \ a_{39}$$

$$a_0 = 0, a_i = 1, 2 \text{ for } i = 1, 2, \ldots 39$$

Correctly represents

$$2^0 \ a_0 + 2^{-1} \ a_1 + \ldots + 2^{-39} \ a_{39}.$$

5

Addition of two such numbers performed in the arithmetic unit will lose the carry from the zero position since there is no place for this carry to go. The arithmetic unit carries out addition of positive numbers modulo 2, that is, the answer is correct except possibly for some added multiple of 2. Note that any adder with a fixed number n of places adds only modulo some number m. The value of m depends on the position of the "decimal" point and can be at most b^n, where b is the base of the number system.

The machine representation $\bar{x}$ of numbers x in the range $-1 \leq x < 1$ is uniquely determined by the fact that addition is performed correctly modulo 2 and the fact that any real number agrees modulo 2 with one and only one number $\bar{x}$ between 0 and 2. If x is restricted to the range given above then there will be only one x corresponding to a machine number $\bar{x}$. The method of determining the representation of any number x is then to find an s such that $\bar{x} = x + 2s$ is in the range 0 to 2 and to digitalize $\bar{x}$. For x in the range $0 \leq x < 1$, $s = 0$, $\bar{x} = x$, and for x in the range $-1 \leq x < 0$ $s = 1$ and $\bar{x} = x + 2$. That is, negative numbers x have an $\bar{x}$ between 1 and 2.

Thus the positive number

$$x = 2^{-1} a_1 + 2^{-2} a_2 + \ldots 2^{-39} a_{39}$$

has the machine representation

$$\bar{x} = x = 0.a_1 a_2 \ldots a_{39}$$

The negative number

$$x = -(2^{-1} a_1 + 2^{-2} a_2 + \ldots + 2^{-39} a_{39})$$

6

has the machine representation

$$\bar{x} = x + 2 = x + 2^0 + 2^{-1} + \dots + 2^{-39} + 2^{-39}$$
$$= 2^0 + (1 - a_1) 2^{-1} + (1 - a_2) 2^{-2} + \dots + (1-a_{39}) 2^{-39} + 2^{-39}$$
$$= 2^0 + 2^{-1} b_1 + 2^{-2} b_2 + \dots + 2^{-39} b_{39} + 2^{-39}$$

where $b_i = 1 - a_i$ (i = 1, 2, ... 39).

That is, the machine representation of $-(2^{-1} a_1 + \dots + 2^{-39} a^{39})$ is obtained from the machine representations of $(2^{-1} a_1 + \dots + 2^{-39} a_{39})$ by changing every 0 digit into a 1 digit (including the sign digit), adding a one to the last place and performing all the carries involved. For example, the machine representation of

$$-1/8 = -(0.001) \text{ is}$$
$$2 - 1/8 = 1.111 = \overline{-1 + 7/8}$$

Binary Decimal Numbers. The Teletype equipment used in ORDVAC furnishes an automatic conversion between the decimal number system and the binary - decimal one as well as the inverse conversion. The latter number system is one in which each decimal digit is replaced by its binary equivalent as follows:

DECIMAL	BINARY
0	0000
1	0001
2	0010
3	0011
4	0100
5	0101
6	0110
7	0111
8	1000
9	1001

The binary-decimal equivalent of any m digit decimal
number is then a 4 m digit binary number obtained by replacing
each decimal digit by its binary equivalent and preserving the
order of the digits. Thus, for example, the binary decimal equivalent of

$$5389$$

is

$$0101 \qquad 0011 \qquad 1000 \qquad 1001$$

The conversion referred to above is accomplished as follows:
The teletypewriter and perforator have been modified so that only
15 keys, a zero bar and two space bars are left on the typewriter.
When a key labeled with a decimal digit is depressed the perforator
cuts a row of holes into the tape, the number and position of the
holes in the row being determined by the number and position of the
digits in the binary equivalent of the decimal digit on the key.
A space is indicated by five holes (ones) on the tape. The letters
K S N J F L are used to represent the binary numbers 1010, 1011, 1100,
1101, 1110, 1111, whose decimal equivalents are 10, 11, 12, 13, 14,
15 respectively. Figure 1.1 shows a tape with the numbers from 0
to 15.

Conversely one may convert from the binary-decimal representation of numbers to the decimal one by supplying instructions to the
teletypewriter in binary decimal form and having the teletypewriter
print the corresponding decimal digit.

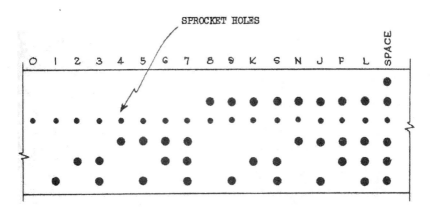

ORDVAC Input Tape

Figure 1.1

1.3 THE ARITHMETIC UNIT Before describing the algorithms used in ORDVAC for performing the various arithmetic operations we shall list some of the properties of the arithmetic unit. A block diagram is shown in Figure 2.1 of Chapter 2.

The Accumulator Register R_1 consists of 40 flipflops. With the similar register R^1 and gates for transferring digits back and forth

9

to R^1, it makes up the double register R_I. Because by using R^1, its contents can be shifted left or right, R_1 is a <u>shifting register.</u>

R_1 is the register which ultimately receives sums from the adder, although these come via R^1. It is the only register whose contents can be sent to the memory. It also receives the contents of the input tape.

Everything that is done by R_1 is achieved by using a sequence of clearing and gating operations. Thus the "language" of the accumulator register and the registers to be described below is that of clears and gates. The detailed organization of the registers will be given in Chapter 2, where it will be shown how the properties of the registers listed in the preceding paragraph may be achieved from a sequence of clearing and gating operations.

The Arithmetic Register R_2 is a structural duplicate of the accumulator register. It, the register R^2 and certain gates make up the double register R_{II}. The registers R_1 and R_2 are interconnected by means of R^1 and R^2 and gates so that certain digits lost in one of these by shifting may be stored in the other. Like R_1, R_2 is a shifting register. It can receive numbers from the memory and its contents can be sent to the number register R^3 or to the output printer or tape punch.

The Number Register R^3 is a single bank of 40 flipflops with gates and clears. It can accept digits from R_2 or from the memory and can transmit its contents to the adder either directly or via a component called the <u>complement gate.</u> This latter device gives the

10

complement of every digit to the adder - digit resolver complex and inserts a carry into the least significant stage of the adder as is required in order to form x - y by the process $\bar{x} + (\overline{-y})$. Thus the machine representation of -y is represented in the adder by reading the digitwise complement of y in R^3 through the complement gate and inserting in the adder the 2^{-39} required.

The Number Register R^3, with the Order Register R_3, makes up R_{III}. However, there is no connection between R_3 and R^3 and R_{III} is not a double register. No shifting occurs here. The order register receives orders from the memory and is a part of the control.

The adder-digit resolver complex forms the sum modulo 2 of a number in the accumulator and a number in the number register and presents this sum to R^1 which may receive it when certain gates are opened.

1.4 ARITHMETIC OPERATIONS. All of the arithmetic operations of ORDVAC are automatic in the sense that a single order is required for each one and the sequencing is then automatically programmed.

Addition and Subtraction. If the augend (minuend) is in the accumulator and the addend (subtrahend) is in the number register then the output of the digit resolver presents the sum (or difference depending on whether the complement gate is not or is used) to the accumulator via its upper set of flipflops, R^1.

Doubling and Halving of Numbers. The machine representation of 2x and x/2 is obtained from that of x by a shifting to the left

11

and right respectively of the digits representing x but special arrangements must be made for the sign digits. We shall now discuss this point. If $0 \leq x < 1$ then its machine representation is

$$\bar{x} = x = 2^{-1}a_1 + 2^{-2}a_2 + \ldots + 2^{-39}a_{39} = 0. \; a_1 \; a_2 \ldots a_{39}.$$

The first 40 digits of the machine representation of x/2 are:

$$(\overline{x/2}) = x/2 = 2^0 \; 0 + 2^{-1} \; 0 + 2^{-2}a_1 + \ldots + 2^{-39}a_{38} = 0.0 \; a_1 \; a_2 \ldots a_{38}.$$

However if $-1 \leq x < 0$ the machine representation of x is:

$$\bar{x} = 2 + x = 2^0 + 2^{-1}b_1 + \ldots + 2^{-39}b_{39} + 2^{-39}$$

The first 40 digits of the machine representation of x/2 are:

$$(\overline{x/2}) = 2 + \frac{x}{2} = 1 + 1/2 \; (2+x) = 2^0 1 + 2^{-1}1 + 2^{-2}b_1 + \ldots + 2^{-39}b_{38}.$$

$$= 1.1 \; b_1 \; b_2 \ldots b_{38}.$$

Hence if the contents of the accumulator are $a_0, a_1, \ldots a_{39}$ and these digits are taken to be the digits of the machine representation of a positive or negative number with binary point placed between a_0 and a_1 then the sign and first thirty-nine binary digits of the machine representation of one-half the number are $a_0, a_0, \ldots a_{38}$. The operation of changing the contents of the accumulator in this manner is called the right shift. This is one of the orders that the machine can execute. In this process the digit a_{39} is placed in the first non-sign position of the arithmetic register R_2, and the non-sign digits

of this register are shifted right, the thirty-ninth being lost.
The right shift order is accomplished by the control's directing
a sequence of clears and gates in R_I and R_{II}.

In discussing the doubling of numbers we must restrict our-
selves to numbers in the range $-1/2 \le x < 1/2$ for then and only then
do we have $-1 \le 2$ $x < 1$. If $0 \le x < 1/2$, then its machine representation
is:

$$2^{-2} a_2 + 2^{-3} a_3 + \ldots + 2^{-39} a_{39} = 0.0a_2 a_3 \ldots a_{39},$$

and the machine representation of 2x is:

$$(\overline{2x}) = 2x = 2^{-1} a_2 + 2^{-2} a_3 + \ldots + 2^{-38} a_{39} = 0. a_2 a_3 \ldots a_{39}0.$$

If $-1/2 \le x < 0$ then its machine representation is:

$$\overline{x} = 2 + x = 2^0 + 2^{-1} + 2^{-2} b_2 + \ldots + 2^{-39} b_{39} = 1.1 b_2 b_3 \ldots b_{39}$$

and the machine representation of 2x is:

$$(\overline{2x}) = 2 + 2x = 2(2 + x) - 2 = 2^0 + 2^{-1} b_2 + \ldots + 2^{-38} b_{39} = 1.b_2 \ldots b_{39}0.$$

Therefore the left shift order which replaces the contents $a_0 \, a_1 \ldots$
a_{39} of the accumulator by $a_0 \, a_2 \ldots a_{38}$, 0 (and simultaneously replaces the contents $c_0, c_1, \ldots c_{39}$ of the arithmetic register by
$c_1, c_2 \ldots c_{39} a_1$) correctly gives the machine representation of 2x
for both positive and negative x when x and 2x are in the range $-1 \le x < 1$.

<u>Multiplication.</u> Multiplication is performed by ORDVAC as
a sequence of additions and halvings. This is done automatically
by causing the control to determine a sequence of clear and gate
operations which insure that the required additions (and divisions
by two) are carried out. We shall now review what this latter sequence must be.

In the multiplication of two numbers the machine representation $\bar{x}$ of the multiplier is stored in the arithmetic register R_2,
The machine representation $\bar{y}$ of the multiplicand is stored in R^3,
and R_1 is initially cleared to zero. The product appears in R_1
and R_2. The former register contains the sign and most significant
39 digits, while R_2 contains the least significant digits of the
product, these having been shifted in from R_1 during the multiplication.
The sign digit of R_2 is made zero.

The multiplication process is performed in thirty-nine steps
on each of which the digit in position 2^{-39} of R_2 is inspected. If
$2^{-39}R_2 = 0$, execute a right shift which gives the machine representation of one-half of the number in the accumulator, R_1. If $2^{-39} R_2 = 1$
add the contents of R^3 to R_1 and then execute a right shift. At the
same time shift R_2 which changes the contents of $2^{-39} R_2$. After the
39th step subtract R^3 from R_1 if $2^0 R_2 = 1$, that is, if the multiplier
is negative. Finally make $2^0 R_2 = 0$.

That these rules give the correct product of x and y may be
seen from the following argument. Let the multiplier be $x = 0..a_1 a_2$
$\ldots a_{39}$ and let the multiplicand be y with the machine representation
$\bar{y}$. The product

$$xy = P_{39}$$

14

where

$$\bar{P}_n = (1/2)(\bar{P}_{n-1} + a_{40-n}\bar{y}).$$

The machine representation of xy is then

$$\bar{P}_{39} = (1/2)(\bar{P}_{38} + a_1\bar{y}).$$

However the machine representation of one-half a number is the right shift order applied to the machine representation of the number and the machine representation of the sum of two numbers is the machine sum (modulo 2) of the machine representation of the numbers. Thus

$$xy = \text{Right Shift of } (\bar{P}_{38} + a_1\bar{y}).$$

Since $\bar{P}_{38}$ is formed correctly by the rules this argument shows that the rules give the correct machine representation of the product of a positive or negative multiplicand and a positive multiplier. When x is negative R_2 contains $2 + x$, and the rules form the product of $(1 + x)$ y during the execution of the thirty-nine steps. Hence y must be subtracted in this case.

If the accumulator register R_1 is not cleared before the multiplication starts, then the rules given above will form the machine representation of $xy + 2^{-39}d$ where d is the number in R_1. By choosing d as 2^{-1} the contents of the accumulator become the machine representation of the "rounded off" product of x and y. The insertion of 2^{-n} into the accumulator is one of the orders that ORDVAC can execute.

Division. ORDVAC'S Control can execute a sequence of clears and gates such that if the machine representation $\bar{x}$ of a dividend

15

x is placed in R_1 and if the machine representation $\bar{y}$ of a divisor
y is placed in R^3, then the rounded machine representation of the
quotient $\bar{z}$ appears in R_2 provided $0 < |x|\,|y| < 1$. If these inequalities
are replaced by equalities the results of the execution of a division
are given in Table 1.1.

The remainder is given by the contents of the accumulator
plus twice the sign digit of the dividend, all times 2^{-39}.

Each step of the division process consists of an addition
(or subtraction) and a left shift of accumulator and arithmetic register. In any one problem the machine always adds or always sub-
tracts. There is no intermixing of addition and subtraction. The
quotient is fed into the arithmetic register R_2 digitwise from the
right hand end. Because the quotient (counting the sign) has 40 digits
while the division takes only 39 steps, the last digit is always made
equal to 1. This is the roundoff.

To perform a division by this method it is necessary to sense
the signs of three quantities:

      (1) Divisor (which is in R^3)

      (2) Dividend (which is in R_1)

      (3) Tentative Partial Remainder (abbreviated as TPR)

The tentative partial remainder is the content of the digit
resolver at the end of any step of the division process. Depending
upon certain conditions it may be used (accepted) or not used (rejected).
If it is accepted, it is shifted left and becomes the true partial
remainder. If it is rejected, the true partial remainder is the

16

accumulator content shifted left one place.

The rules are as follows:

    (1) If the signs of divisor and dividend

        (a) <u>agree, subtract</u> throughout the process.

        (b) <u>disagree, add</u> throughout the process.

    (2) If the signs of tentative partial remainder and dividend

        (a) <u>agree, accept</u> TPR by transferring digit resolver content, shifted left one place, into R_1.

        (b) <u>disagree, reject</u> TPR by not using digit resolver content and simply shifting R_1 content left one place.

    (3) If the signs of tentative partial remainder and divisor

        (a) <u>agree</u>, insert 1 as quotient digit into right hand end of R_2 and shift left with R_1.

        (b) <u>disagree</u>, insert 0 as quotient digit into right hand end of R_2 and shift left with R_1.

That these rules lead to the result claimed may be seen as follows: Let $\bar{r}_n$ be the contents of R_1 at the end of the nth step with $\bar{r}_0 = \bar{x}$ and let $\bar{t}_n$ be the digit resolver output during this step. The quantity $\bar{r}_{39}$ is sometimes referred to as the <u>residue</u>. Then

17

SPECIAL CASES FOR DIVISION

Let x = dividend, y = divisor

	DIVIDEND	DIVISOR	QUOTIENT
CASE I	> 0	> 0	$-1 + 2^{-39}$
$0 < \|x\| = \|y\| < 1$	< 0	> 0	$-1 + 2^{-39}$
	> 0	< 0	$1 - 2^{-39}$
	< 0	< 0	$1 - 2^{-39}$
CASE II	> 0	-1	Digitwise comple-
$\|x\| < 1, y = -1$	< 0	-1	ment of dividend except for roundoff
CASE III	> 0	0	Digitwise comple-
$0 \leq \|x\| < 1, y = 0$	< 0	0	ment of dividend except for roundoff
CASE IV	-1	0	$1 - 2^{-39}$
CASE V	-1	-1	$1 - 2^{-39}$

Table 1.1

18

$$\bar{t}_n = (\bar{r}_{n-1} - (-1)^{d_0' + a_0}\,\bar{y})\bmod 2$$

$$\bar{r}_n = 2\,\bar{r}_{n-1}\bmod 2 \text{ if } a_0 + b_n = 1$$

$$= 2\,\bar{t}_n\bmod 2 \text{ if } a_0 + b_n = 0,2$$

where a_0 is the sign digit of $\bar{x}$, b_n is the sign digit of $\bar{t}_n$, and d_0 is the sign digit of $\bar{y}$.

The formula of $\bar{r}_n$ may be written as

$$\bar{r}_n = \left[2\left\{ 1/2\,(1(-1)^{a_0 + b_n})\bar{r}_{n-1} + 1/2\,(1 + (-1)^{a_0 + b_n}\bar{t}_n\} \right]\bmod 2.$$

We next define a number $r_{n-1} = \bar{r}_{n-1} + 2\,a_0$. Note that $\left|r_{n-1}\right|$ may exceed unity and hence that $\bar{r}_{n-1}$ is not necessarily its machine representation. If $\left|\bar{r}_{n-1}\right| < 1$, then $\bar{r}_{n-1}$ is its machine representation. We now consider

$$\bar{t}_n = (r_{n-1} + 2\,a_0 - (-1)^{d_0 + a_0}(y + 2\,d_0)) \bmod 2.$$

We shall prove later that all r_n have the same signs as the dividend. It may be readily verified by examining the four cases involved that if $b_n = 1 - a_0$ (the tentative partial remainder is rejected), then

$$\left|r_{n-1}\right| < y < 1.$$

If $b_n = a_0$ (the tentative partial remainder is accepted, then $\left|y\right| < \left|r_{n-1}\right| < 2\ \left|y\right| < 2$. Therefore if the tentative partial remainder is rejected $\bar{r}_{n-1}$ is the machine representation of r_{n-1} whose sign is the same as that of the dividend. Thus we always have

$$\bar{r}_n = 2\left[1/2\,(-1\,(-1)^{a_0 + b_n})\,\bar{r}_{n-1} + 1/2\,(1 + (-1)^{a_0 + b_n}\bar{t}) \right] - 2a_0.$$

By using the results given above and further examining the cases it may be verified that

$$1/2(1 + (-1)^{a_0+b}n)\ \bar{t}_n = 1/2(1 + (-1)^{a_0+b}n)(r_{n-1} + 2a_0 - (-1)^{d_0+a_0}(y+2d_0)$$

$$-2(-1)^{a_0}\ d_0).$$

Hence by substitution in the formula for $\bar{r}_n$ we have

$$r_n = 2r_{n-1} - (-1)^{d_0+a_0}(1 + (-1)^{a_0+b}n)\ y.$$

It follows from this by an induction argument that the signs of r_n and r_0 are the same, for the sign of r_n is that of r_{n-1} or that of t_n, whose machine representation is $\bar{t}_n$. The latter case can occur only if the sign of $\bar{t}_n$ is that of $\bar{x}$.

Successive substitution in this formula gives

$$2^{-39}\ r_{39} = r_0 - (-1)^{d_0+a_0}y\ \sum_{i=1}^{39} 2^{-i}\left[1 + (-1)^{a_0+b_i}\right]$$

$$= r_0 - (-1)^{d_0+a_0}y\ (1-2^{-39}) - (-1)^{d_0}y\sum_{i=1}^{39} 2^{-i}\ (-1)^{b_i}.$$

The rules for forming the quotient digits insure that the contents of R_2 at the end of the nth step are

$$\bar{z}_n = \sum_{i=1}^{n} 2^{-38+n-i}\qquad q_{i-1} = \sum_{i=1}^{n} 2^{-39+n-i}\left[1 + (-1)^{d_0+ b_i}\right]$$

where $\quad q_{i=1} = 1/2\left[1 + (-1)^{d_0+b_i}\right]$

20

Note that

$$q_0 = 1/2 \left[1 + (-1)^{d_0+b_1}\right] = 1/2 \left[1 - (-1)^{d_0+a_0}\right]$$

since the first partial remainder is always rejected because $|y| > |r_0|$. The digit q_0 is the correct sign digit for the quotient.

The final number in R_2 is

$$\bar{z} = \bar{z}_{39} + 2^{-39} q_{39} = \bar{z}_{39} + 2^{-39}$$

since our rules are to insert a 1 in the last digit of the quotient. In general we have

$$\bar{z} = \sum_{i=1}^{39} 2^{-i} \left[1 + (-1)^{d_0+b_i}\right] + 2^{-39} q_{39}$$

$$= 1 - 2^{-39} + 2^{-39} q_{39} + (-1) \sum_{i=1}^{39} 2^{-i} (-1)^{b_i}.$$

The number represented by $\bar{z}$ is

$$z = \bar{z} - 2q_0 = 1 - 2q_0 - 2^{-39}(1 - q_{39}) + (-1)^{d_0} \sum_{i=1}^{39} 2^{-i} (-1)^{b_i}.$$

Substituting from this into the expression for $2^{-39} r_{39}$ we get

$$2^{-39} r_{39} = r_0 - (-1)^{d_0+a_0} y(1 - 2^{-39}) + y (1-2q_0 - 2^{-39}(1-q_{39}) - z).$$

That is

$$zy + 2^{-39} r_{39} = x + 2^{-39} y (q_{39} - 2q_0)$$

$$= r_0 + 2^{-39} y (1-2q_0).$$

From this identity it is evident that $z - 2^{-39} (1 - 2q_0)$ is the quotient and $2^{-39}r_{39}$ is the remainder relative to this quotient. That is, $2^{-39} (\bar{r}_{39} + 2a_0)$ is the remainder relative to this quotient. This identity may be interpreted in another way: z may be called the rounded quotient and relative to this quotient

$$2^{-39} (r_{39} - (1 - 2q_0) y) = 2^{-39}(\bar{r}_{39} + 2a_0 - (1 - 2q_0) y)$$

is the remainder.

1.5 <u>EXAMPLES OF ARITHMETIC OPERATIONS.</u> In this section we shall use a five digit machine to illustrate the machine representation of numbers and the machine's methods of performing the arithmetic operations on numbers.

If $x = 3/16$ then $\bar{x} = .0011$,

$-x = -3/16$ and $(\overline{-x}) = 1.1101 = 1 + 13/16$,

If $y = 4/16$ then $\bar{y} = .0100$,

$-y = -4/16$ and $(\overline{-y}) = 1.1100 = 1 + 12/16$.

If x and y are the numbers given above, then $x + y$ and $x - y$ are formed as follows:

$\bar{x} + \bar{y}$:

$$
\begin{array}{l}
0.0011 \\
0.0100 \\
\hline
0.0111 = \overline{(x + y)} = 7/16
\end{array}
$$

$\bar{x} + (\overline{-y})$:

$$
\begin{array}{l}
.0011 \\
1.1100 \\
\hline
1.1111 = \overline{(x - y)} = -1/16
\end{array}
$$

Note that

$$(\overline{-x}) + (\overline{-y}) \text{ mod } 2 = 1.1101$$
$$\underline{1.1100}$$
$$\overline{1.1001} = \overline{[-(x+y)]} = 1 + 9/16$$

For the purpose of illustrating multiplication of x = multiplier and (-y) = multiplicand, we shall show the state of the registers R_1 and R_2 at the end of each of the four steps. At the beginning we have:

R_1 : 0 0 0 0 0

R_2 : 0 0 0 1 1

R^3 : 1 1 1 0 0

The register R^3 is never altered. At the end of the first step (after adding $R_1 + R^3$ mod 2 and halving):

R_1 : 1 1 1 1 0

R_2 : 0 0 0 0 1

At the end of the second step (after adding $R_1 + R^3$ mod 2 and halving)

R_1 : 1 1 1 0 1

R_2 : 0 0 0 0 0

At the end of the third step (after halving only, since $2^{-4} R_2 = 0$)

R_1 : 1 1 1 1 0

R_2 : 0 1 0 0 0

and at the end of the fourth step (after halving only since $2^{-4}R_2 = 0$)

R_1 : 1 1 1 1 1

R_2 : 0 0 1 0 0

The result of the multiplication has the binary expansion 1.1 1 1 1 0 1 00 = 1 + 61/64 which is the machine representation of -3/64 = -12/256 = -3/16 x 4/16.

If a rounded multiplication had been performed, the R_1 register would have initially contained 0.1 0 0 0 and the steps would have proceeded as before. The result in R_1 would have been 1.1 1 1 1 = -1/16 = -4/64.

We shall now form x/ (-y) in accordance with the rules by the machine: Initially we have

R^3: 1 1 1 0 0

R_1: 0 0 0 1 1

R_2: 0 0 0 0 0 (See Note)

The first tentative partial remainder is

$\bar{t}_1$= 1. 1 1 1 1.

Since the sign digit of this differs from that of the contents of R_1, t_1 is rejected. Further, since this agrees with the sign digit of R^3, the first quotient digit is 1. Hence at the end of this step we have

R_1: 0 0 1 1 0

R_2: 0 0 0 1 0

The second tentative partial remainder is

$\bar{t}_2$ = 0. 0 0 1 0.

Hence $\bar{t}_2$ is accepted and the quotient digit is zero.

R_1: 0 0 1 0 0

R_2: 0 0 1 0 0

The third tentative partial remainder is

$$\bar{t}_3 = 0. \ 0 \ 0 \ 0 \ 0$$

which is accepted, and the quotient digit is zero. Hence

R_1: 0 0 0 0 0

R_2: 0 1 0 0 0

the fourth tentative partial remainder is

$$\bar{t}_4 = 1.1 \ 1 \ 0 \ 0$$

which is rejected and which gives a quotient digit of 1. Hence

R_1: 0 0 0 0 0

R_2: 1 0 0 1 1

The last one in R_2 is inserted in accordance with the round-off procedure.

The rounded quotient then is

$$z = -13/16,$$

the actual quotient being -12/16. The remainder is in this case zero. This is the true remainder.

NOTE: The register R_2 is not actually cleared, but as the quotient is shifted in from the right the previous contents are lost by overflowing from the left end.

1.6 THE CODE. The list of orders that ORDVAC can execute is called the code. A partial list of these orders is given and described in Section 1.8. It is the purpose of this section to give a general description of these orders.

ORDVAC is a one address machine. That is, each order
that ORDVAC can execute refers at most to a single address. For
example a typical order reads: add the absolute value of the number
at position 5 in the memory to the number in the accumulator (leaving
the result in the accumulator). Therefore each order when stored
in the memory of ORDVAC requires at least 10 digits for the address
digits involved in that order. Another nine digits called the instruction digits are used to describe the order to ORDVAC.

Orders are stored in the memory in pairs. That is, a given
address in the memory which contains 40 digits either contains a
pair of orders or a number. These may be interlaced in any fashion.
No portion of the memory is reserved exclusively for orders or exclusively for numbers and hence in some instances order pairs may be
used as operands for arithmetic operations. ORDVAC may by this means
modify its own instructions in accordance with a prescribed plan.
A single order consists of 20 digits (one being a blank): the digits
0 to 8 (or 20 to 28) describe the instruction, digit 9 or 29 is not
used and the digits 10 to 19 (or 30 to 39) describe the address of
the number involved in the order if the order deals with a number.
In the case of the shift orders or the control transfer orders (see
below) and some additional orders the address portion of the order
is used for other purposes.

When pairs of orders are brought out of the memory they are

stored in the order register R_3.

In addition to orders relating to the operations of arithmetic ORDVAC has orders which transfer sets of digits within the arithmetic unit and among the various parts of the machine. These can be described by listing each register of the arithmetic unit and relating entrances and exits to the register. A list of orders is given in Section 1.8.

The accumulator R_1 may receive information from the digit resolver via R^1 in a parallel fashion and from the input in a serial fashion. It may transfer its contents wholly or partially to the memory in a parallel fashion. It may exchange information with R_2 by shifting. The addition order is involved implicitly or explicitly in getting information into R_1 in a parallel fashion. The store orders (M and E, E') are used to get information from R_1 to the memory. By using the orders E or E' ORDVAC can be made to change its orders. The tape order is used to transfer information from the input to R_1. This is the only automatic entrance for information ORDVAC can use.

The arithmetic register R_2 can receive information from the memory by the R order and from R_1 by shifting. Its contents may determine the contents of R_1 by using the A orders and by shifting. In the A orders R^3 and the adder are used. The contents of R_2 may be given to the output in a serial fashion by the P (print) order.

The number register R^3 obtains information from the memory and from R_2. It is used in the execution of a number of orders such as

27

addition, multiplication and division. In the execution of such orders its information is placed in the adder.

There is another inportant class of orders that ORDVAC has. These are the control transfer orders. Normally ORDVAC executes an order pair described by digits at a location n in the memory and then goes to position n + 1 for its next order pair. This process may be changed by the use of the control transfer orders. The unconditional control transfer orders interrupt this process under all conditions whereas the conditional orders do so only if the contents of R_1 represent a non-negative number. The presence of the conditional transfer order makes possible the use of ORDVAC for solving problems involving iterative routines of variable length.

1.7 THE CONTROL. The functions of the control are: to decide which order is to be executed and to supervise the execution of the order, noting when it has been completed. In order to perform the first function the control has a counter called the control counter which contains the address of the next order pair to be executed. We shall describe the operation of the control assuming that the second order of an order pair has been executed, that this order was not a control transfer order, and that the address of the next order pair is in the control counter.

The control then consults the memory for the information stored at this address and places this information in the order register R_3. The information may not be immediately available from the memory since the memory may be regenerating. However at the end

28

of one regeneration period and before the next one occurs the control can require a transfer from the address in the control counter to R_3. The control counter is advanced by one after the memory is consulted.

Once the information is in R_3 the control begins the execution of the order described by the digits 0 through 19 (the left hand order). The instruction digits in R_3 go to a register R_4, the decoding register, which decodes the instruction and sets the sequence of gates and clears desired. The address portion of the order, digits 10 to 19 goes to the address generator of the memory, to the control counter, or to a recognition circuit. See Drawing 266. The destination depends on the values of the digits 0 to 8. Let us suppose that the first possibility takes place. Then the number stored at the address described by the digits 10 to 19 in R_3 is brought out of the memory and placed in R^3 in accordance with the instruction. The control then executes the sequences of gates and clears in the registers of the arithmetic unit necessary to carry out the instruction. In case the address digits go to the order counter a control transfer is made after the execution of the instruction. The address digits go to the recognition circuit in the case of orders involving shifts.

After the order described by digits 0 to 19 is executed, and if it was not a control transfer order, the order described by digits 20 to 39, the right-hand order, is dealt with. The address digits are first transferred to position 10 to 19 and the instruction digits are sent to R_4. The process described above for the left-hand order

29

then takes place. When this is completed the control begins again
with the order pair stored at the address in the order counter.
This address will be one greater than the previous one unless
the order counter has been modified in the execution of an order
pair.

1.8 THE LIST OF ORDERS. The list of orders currently being used on ORDVAC (which does not comprise all orders possible) is described below. Every complete order may be represented as a 5 sexadecimal digit number which is the sum of a two or three digit instruction and a 3 digit address. The following list shows the left hand 2 (or in some cases 3) digits of the instruction. The remaining digits of the instruction are zero.

If the instruction is given with two digits, formation of the complete order is trivally simple since the addition of the address merely gives a 5 digit number made up of the instruction digits followed by the address digits. Example: Consider order 19 with the decimal address 526. The complete order is then 7J20F where 20F is the sexadecimal representation of 526.

If the instruction is given with 3 digits, the addition of instruction and address must be carried out. Example: Consider order 9 with the decimal address 526. The complete order is then FO800 + 20F = FOKOF.

TABLE 1.2

LIST OF ORDERS

ORDER	SYMBOL	SEXADECIMAL REPRESENTATION	
1.	+ x	L5	Clear R_1 and add number at memory location x into R_1.
2.	- x	L1	Clear R_1 and subtract number at memory location x into R_1.

ORDER	SYMBOL	SEXADECIMAL REPRESENTATION	
3.	$|+|x$	L7	Clear R_1 and add absolute value of number at memory location x into R_1.
4.	$|-|x$	L3	Clear R_1 and subtract absolute value of number at location x into R_1.
5.	$(+)x$	L4	Same as 1 without clearing R_1.
6.	$(-)x$	L0	Same as 2 without clearing R_1.
7.	$[+]x$	L6	Same as 3 without clearing R_1.
8.	$[-]x$	L2	Same as 4 without clearing R_1.
9.	Rx	F08	Clear R_2 and add number at memory location x into R_2.
10.	A + x	358	Clear R_1 and add number R_2 into R_1. *If this is a right hand order, transfer control to the left hand order at memory location x. If this is a left hand order, do the right hand order and then transfer control to the left hand order at memory location x.
11.	A - x	318	Clear R_1 and subtract number in R_2 into R_1. *Repeat as in 10.
12.	$A|+|x$	378	Clear R_1 and add absolute value of number in R_2 into R_1. *Repeat as in 10.
13.	$A|-|x$	338	Clear R_1 and subtract absolute value of number in R_2 into R_1. *Repeat as in 10.

14.	A(+)x	348	Same as 10 without clearing R_1.

| 15. | A(-)x | 308 | Same as 11 without clearing R_1. |

| 16. | A $\left[+\right]$x | 368 | Same as 12 without clearing R_1. |

| 17. | A $\left[-\right]$x | 328 | Same as 13 without clearing R_1. |

18. Xux 75 Clear R_1; multiply the number in R_2 by the number at memory location x, putting the sign and 39 most significant digits of the product in R_1 and the 39 least significant digits of the product in the right hand 39 digits of R_2. Make the sign digit of R_2 equal to 0.

19. Xx 7J Clear R_1 and insert 2^{-1} into R_1. Then follow 18.

20. (X)x   Do not clear R_1. Then follow 18.

21. $\div$ x 66 Clear R_2 and divide the number in R_1 by the number at memory location x. Place the quotient in R_2 and the remainder in R_1. Always make 2^{-39} $R_2 = 1$.

22. ←n 00 If n = 0, the machine will not proceed. If $0 < n \leq 63$ do n times the left shift operation which replaces the contents $\epsilon_0 \epsilon_1 \epsilon_2 \ldots \epsilon_{39}$ of R_1 and $\pi_0 \pi_1 \pi_2 \cdots \pi_{39}$ of R_2 by $\epsilon_0 \epsilon_2 \epsilon_3 \ldots \epsilon_{39}$ 0 and $\pi_1 \pi_2 \pi_3 \cdots \pi_{39} \epsilon_1$.

23. ⟨∕n 09 If n = 0, the machine will not proceed. If $0 < n \leq 63$, clear R_1, insert 2^{-1} in R_1, and do the left shift operation n times.

24. ←0 01 If n = 0, the machine will not proceed. If $0 < n \leq 63$, clear R_1 and do the left shift operation n times.

25.	→ n	10	If n ≠ 0, the machine will not proceed. If $0 < n \leq 63$, do n times the right shift operation which replaces the contents $\epsilon_0 \epsilon_1 \epsilon_2 \ldots \epsilon_{39}$ of R_1 and $\pi_0 \pi_1 \pi_2 \ldots \pi_{39}$ of R_2 by $\epsilon_0 \epsilon_0 \epsilon_1 \ldots \epsilon_{38}$ and $\pi_0 \epsilon_{39} \pi_1 \pi_2 \ldots \pi_{38}$.
26.	⇥ n	19	If n ≠ 0, the machine will not proceed. If $0 < n \leq 63$, clear R_1, insert 2^{-1} in R_1, and do the right shift operation n times.
27.	⊖ n	11	If n ≠ 0, the machine will not proceed. If $0 < n \leq 63$, clear R_1 and do the right shift operation n times.
28.	U x	24	Transfer control to the left hand order of the word at memory location x.
29.	OUx	25	Clear R_1. Then transfer control to the left hand order at memory location x.
30.	U'x	K0	Transfer control to the right hand order of the word at memory location x.
31.	OU'x	K1	Clear R_1. Then transfer control to the right hand order at memory location x.
32.	C x	28	If the number in R_1 is ≥ 0, follow 28. Otherwise do nothing and proceed to next order.
33.	C'x	22	If the number in R_1 is ≥ 0, follow 30. Otherwise do nothing and proceed to next order.
34.	M x	40	Store the contents of R_1 at memory location x. Do not change R_1.
35.	OMx	41	Store 0 at memory location x.
36.	1Mx	49	Store 1/2 at memory location x.
37.	Ex	46	Replace digits 2^{-10} through 2^{-19} of memory location x by the corresponding digits of R_1. Do not change R_1.

| 38. | OEx | 47 | Clear R_1. Then do the E operation. |

38. OEx 47 Clear R_1. Then do the E operation.

39. E'x 42 Replace digits 2^{-30} through 2^{-39} of memory location x by the corresponding digits of R_1. Do not change R_1.

40. OE'x 43 Clear R_1. Then do the E' operation.

41. P 80828 Print the contents of R_2 on the teletype, (destroying the contents of R_1 and R_2 in the process).

42. T 80028 Read one word from the input tape into R_1, (Changing R_2 in the process).

43. Zx 30 Stop the computer. If this is a right hand order, transfer control to left hand order at memory location x when starting again. If this is a left hand order, when starting again do the right hand order and then transfer control. The stop part of this order can be ignored by setting a switch on the control panel, in which case the order becomes a transfer order.

44. Zu 20 Stop the computer.

45. FO FO Replace the contents $\epsilon_0\ \epsilon_1\ ..\ \epsilon_{39}$ of R_1 and $\pi_0\ \pi_1\ ...\pi_{39}$ of R_2 by $\epsilon_1\ \epsilon_2\ ...\epsilon_{39}$ π_1 and $\pi_0\ \pi_2\ ...\pi_{39}\ \pi_{40}$ respectively, where π_{40} is the same as π_{39} was prior to the last order which used a right shift. (This would be any of the addition, multiplication, A, or right shift orders),

46. OFO F1 Clear R_1 and do the FO order.

47. 1FO F9 Clear R_1, insert 2^{-1} in R_1, and do the FO order.

48. KO8x KO8 Do the FO order and transfer control to memory location x when the right hand order has been executed.

| 49. | 0K08x | K18 | Clear R_1 and do the K08 order. |
| 50. | 1K08x | K98 | Clear R_1, insert 2^{-1} in R_1 and do the K08 order. |

1.9 SQUARE ROOT ROUTINE. In this section we shall illustrate the use of the orders listed above by listing a sequence of orders for the solution of the following problem: The machine representation of a positive number $a < 1$ is stored at memory location P; compute $\sqrt{a}$ and place it at memory location q.

Mathematical Analysis. The square root is achieved by a succession of approximations given by the formula,

$$z_{i+1} = (1/2)(z_i + a/z_i)$$

Of course the machine does not carry out the operations indicated exactly. This fact must be taken into account in examining the error in the square root. It may readily be verified from this equation that

$$z_{i+1}^2 - a = \frac{1}{4z_i^2}(z_i^2 - a)^2,$$

That is, the error is essentially squared on each iteration if division is an exact operation. Moreover we have

$$z_{i+1} - \sqrt{a} = \frac{1}{2z_i}(\sqrt{a} - z_i)^2 > 0$$

$$z_{i+1} - z_i = 1/2\left(\frac{a}{z_i} - z_i\right) = \frac{1}{2z_i}(a - z_i^2)$$

37

Hence if $z_1 > a$ we will have

$$z_1 > z_2 > \cdots \quad z_i > z_{i+1} > \sqrt{a}.$$

Thus the sequence of approximants to the square root will be greater than the square root if the operations are carried out exactly.

However machine operations such as division and halving (division by 2) are not carried out exactly. Moreover a rounded division can be carried out correctly only if the divisor is greater than the dividend. Hence in order to use the algorithim described above we must rewrite it in a form suitable for machine computation. The form we use is

$$\overline{z}_{i+1} = \overline{z}_i + (\overline{a} \div \overline{z}_i - \overline{z}_i) \div 2$$

where the bar denotes the machine representation of a number the $\div$ sign denotes machine division and $\div 2$ represents machine halving. We shall verify that if $0 \le \overline{a} < 1 - 2^{-39}$ the sequence of numbers obtained by setting $z_1 = 1 - 2^{-39}$ and using this formula have the property that $z_i > z_{i+1} > \sqrt{a}$ for values of i less than some value $i_0 > 1$.   Moreover for i_0 defined by $\overline{z}_{i_0+1} \ge \overline{z}_{i_0}$, $\overline{z}_{i_0}$ is the approximate square root of a in the sense that $\left| \overline{z}_{i_0} - \sqrt{a} \right| \le 2^{-38}$. Before deriving these results we note that

$$\left| (a/b - \overline{a}) \right| + \overline{b} \le 2^{-39}$$

38

$$\left|\left(\frac{a}{2} - a\right) + 2\right| \le 2^{-40}$$

as is evident from the division algorithm and the process of halving. It is a consequence of these round-off errors that

$$\bar{z}_{i+1} = 1/2 \ \left(\bar{z}_i + \frac{\bar{a}}{\bar{z}_i}\right) + r$$

with

$$|r| \le 2^{-39}.$$

Hence

$$\bar{z}_{i+1} - \sqrt{a} - r = \frac{1}{2\bar{z}_i} (\bar{z}_i - a)^2 > 0.$$

That is, we always have

$$\bar{z}_{i+1} > \sqrt{a} \ -2^{-39}.$$

Suppose first that

$$\bar{a} < \sqrt{\bar{a}} \ + 2^{-38} < z_i \le 1 - 2^{-39}.$$

Then

$$a < \frac{\bar{a}}{\bar{z}_i} < \sqrt{\bar{a}}$$

and $\bar{a} \div \bar{z}_i$ is a positive digital number. Moreover

$$\bar{z}_i - (\bar{a} \div \bar{z}_i) = (\bar{z}_i - \sqrt{\bar{a}}) + (\sqrt{\bar{a}} - (\bar{a}/\bar{z}_i)) + \bar{a}/\bar{z}_i - (\bar{a} \div \bar{z}_i) > 2^{-39}$$

as follows from the replacement of each parenthesis by its smallest possible value. Therefore

$$(\bar{z}_i - \bar{a} \div \bar{z}_i) \div 2 \geq 2^{-39}$$

and

$$z_{i+1} \leq \bar{z}_i - 2^{-39} < \bar{z}_i.$$

Hence values of i such that $\bar{z}_i$ are in the range given above are less than i_o. Suppose now that

$$\sqrt{\bar{a}} - 2^{-39} < \bar{z}_i \leq \sqrt{\bar{a}} + 2^{-38}$$

Then we may write

$$\bar{z}_i = \sqrt{\bar{a}} + S2^{-39} \quad \text{with} \quad -1 \leq S \leq 2$$

and

$$\frac{\bar{a}}{\bar{z}_i} = \frac{\bar{a}}{\sqrt{\bar{a}} + S2^{-39}} = \sqrt{\bar{a}} - S2^{-39} + \frac{S^2 2^{-78}}{\sqrt{\bar{a}} + S2^{-39}}$$

Hence

$$\bar{a} \div \bar{z}_i \geq \bar{a}^{1/2} - S2^{-39} + t 2^{-39}$$

where $t = \pm 1$ and the last term on the right hand side is the error due to the rounded division.

$$\bar{a} \div \bar{z}_i - \bar{z}_i \geq (t - 2S) 2^{-39}$$

If $\quad \bar{a} \div \bar{z}_i - \bar{z}_i \geq 0$ then $\bar{z}_{i+1} \geq \bar{z}_i$ and $i = i_o$.

The quantity $\bar{z}_{i_0}$ is called the machine square root of $\bar{a}$. If $(\bar{a} \div \bar{z}_i) - \bar{z}_i < 0$ then we know that $\sqrt{\bar{a}} - 2^{-39} < \bar{z}_{i+1}$ $< \bar{z}_i < \sqrt{\bar{a}} + 2^{-38}$.

Since every strictly decreasing sequence of digital numbers must be finite we must have a value of $i = i_0$ such that $\bar{a} \div \bar{z}_{i_0} -$ $z_{i_0} \geq 0$ that is, $z_{i_0 + 1} \geq z_{i_0}$.

This can only occur if

$$ - 2^{-29} < (\bar{z}_{i_0} - \sqrt{\bar{a}}) \leq 2^{-38}. $$

There fore this relation is an error estimate for machine square root. The right hand inequality may be sharpened but this will not be done here.

$\underline{\text{The Program.}}$ The algorithm for finding the square root cannot be applied to the case $\bar{a} = 1 - 2^{-39}$ for in that case $\bar{z}_i = \bar{a}$ and $\bar{a} \div \bar{z}_i = -1 + 2^{-39}$ instead of 1 or $1 - 2^{-39}$ which would terminate the process. Therefore the code first tests for this value of $\bar{a}$.

The storage needed (other than orders) is

Address	Contents
r	$1 - 2^{-39}$
p	a
q	z_1

ORDER ADDRESS	ORDER	DESCRIPTION
0	+ p	Accumulator has $\bar{a}$
	(-) r	Accumulator has $\bar{a} - (1 - 2^{-39})$
1	C'6	Control to RH side of 6 if accumulator contents ≥ 0.
	+ r	Accumulator has $\bar{z}_1 = 1 - 2^{-39}$
2	M q	q has $\bar{z}_1$
	+ p	Accumulator has $\bar{a}$
3	÷ q	R_2 has $a \div \bar{z}_1$
	A + 4	Accumulator has $\bar{a} \div \bar{z}_1$; control to 4
4	(-)q	Accumulator has $\bar{a} + \bar{z}_1 - \bar{z}_1$
	C' 7	Control to RH side of 7 if accumulator contents ≥ 0
5	1	Accumulator has $\left[(\bar{a} + \bar{z}_1) - \bar{z}_1 \right] \div 2$
	+ q	Accumulator has $\bar{z}_{i+1} = \left[(\bar{a} + \bar{z}_1) - \bar{z}_1 \right] \div 2 + \bar{z}_1$
6	U 2	Control to LH side of 2
	+ r	Accumulator has $1 - 2^{-39}$
7	M q	q has $1 - 2^{-39} = \sqrt{a}$ in special case
	END	

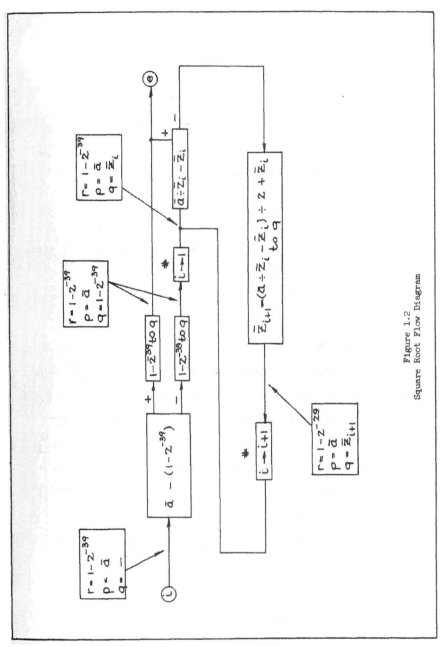

Figure 1.2
Square Root Flow Diagram

43

CHAPTER 2

THE ARITHMETIC UNIT

The arithmetic unit consists of three registers (two of
them double registers) which are essentially storage units for
holding the factors involved in arithmetic operations, a parallel
40 binary digit adder, and other subsidiary units such as the
complement gate which provides the complement of the number in
one of the registers. The three registers, and a fourth which
is part of the control, were constructed as three double registers.
A block diagram of the arithmetic unit is shown in Figure 2.1.

The registers of the arithmetic unit correspond to the
keyboard and dials on the common desk calculator. They hold the
operands while the operations of arithmetic take place, and they
present the results of these operations. The basic components of
the registers are the flipflop and the gate.

2.1 THE FLIPFLOP. The flipflop[#] (or toggle) is based
upon the Eccles-Jordon circuit which, as is well known, has
two stable states. The standard flipflop circuit used in ORDVAC
is shown in Figure 2.2.

By definition the flipflop represents the binary number 1
when the right-hand triode is cut off and the left-hand triode is
conducting.

[#] An equivalent term is **bi-stable multivibrator**

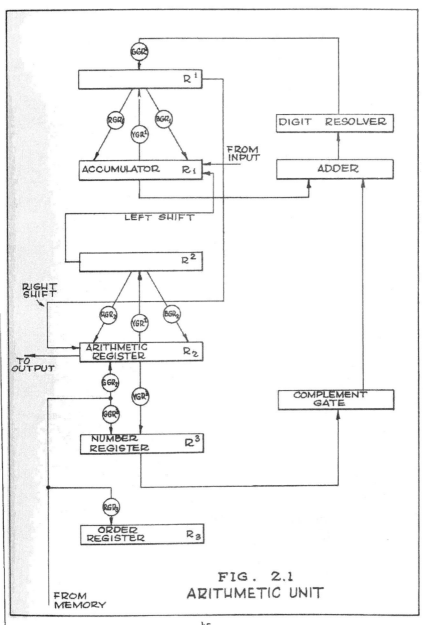

FIG . 2.1
ARITHMETIC UNIT

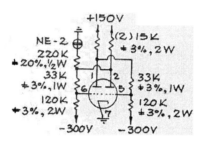

+150V

NE-2
220K
±20%,½W
33K
±3%,1W
120K
±3%,2W

(2)15K
±3%,2W

1   2
6   5
7

33K
±3%,1W

120K
±3%,2W

−300V   −300V

6J6

Figure 2.2 The Flipflop

This means that plate 2 will be high, and the neon will be on.
Typical voltages for the 1 state are given in Fig. 2.3. The voltages
would be interchanged between triodes for the 0 state. The voltage
on grid 5 is usually sensed to determine the state of the flipflop.
If this is done 1 corresponds to -37 volts and 0 corresponds to 0
volts.

2.2 <u>TRANSFER OF INFORMATION</u>. The storing of information
in a flipflop involves changing the state of the flipflop. A change

of state can be achieved by any action which both unbalances the flipflop and moves both triodes into the operating region of their characteristics. Thus one plate supply can be dropped, one plate can be shorted to ground, or one grid voltage can be changed. This will unbalance the flipflop and, if the correct one of the two possible actions is chosen in each case, both triodes will be in the operating regions of their characteristics and a change of state will occur. Changing the state of a flipflop is usually called <u>gating</u> or <u>clearing</u>, the term used depending upon how the change is carried out.

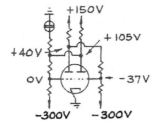

Figure
2.3
Typical Flipflop
Voltages

47

Clearing a Flipflop. The need for "clearing" the flipflop in a register arises from the fact that, for reasons of economy in design, most of the signals available for changing a flipflop are single-ended; i.e., only one wire with two voltage levels, corresponding to 0 and 1, is used. The action on a flipflop by such a signal can be only unilateral. It can be designed to change the toggle from 0 to 1 or from 1 to 0, but it cannot accomplish both actions with the same design. Thus the flipflop must be previously changed to the state which enables the signal to control. This is exactly analogous to the action on a desk calculator. The action of placing numbers on a keyboard is unilateral, since keys are always depressed and never lifted by hand. Prior to depressing the keys, therefore, the keyboard must be "cleared" and all keys released to their "up" positions; otherwise certain unwanted keys would be left "down" from a previous operation.

The clearing action in the ORDVAC register is accomplished by dropping one plate supply voltage from + 150 V to about + 50 V. Dropping the voltage on pin 1 (Fig. 2.2) will place the toggle in a 1 state. Dropping the supply to pin 2 will place the toggle in a 0 state.

Gating a Flipflop. The changing of the flipflop by gating is accomplished by reducing the plate voltage of one plate of the toggle. The reduction in plate voltage is accomplished electronically through a so-called "gate" tube. Thus, in Figure 2.4 if a zero voltage is placed on the gate tube grid, the tube will conduct and pull plate 1 down.

48

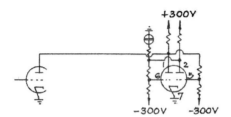

Figure 2.4

Gating a Flipflop

If the toggle had beeñ previously cleared to 0, the resultant action would have been to change the toggle from 0 to 1.

Usually, in addition, it is desired to control the duration of the gate timewise. To do this a further controlling signal can be placed on the cathode of the gate tube. In Fig. 2.5, if a + 10V signal is on the cathode of the tube (6J6), it will not conduct even with the zero grid voltage present. When the cathode is changed to

-10 volts, the tube then conducts and gates the flipflop. The "not
gate" voltage on the grid of the gate tube is made to be -20 V or
less, so that it will not conduct even with -10 V on the cathode.

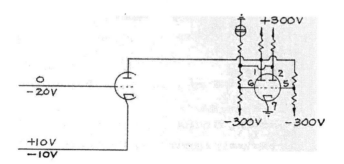

Figure 2.5
Controlled Gating of a Flipflop

Double Gating a Flipflop. It is possible to transfer information without clearing if gates are connected to both sides of
a flipflop. In Fig. 2.6 the contents of flipflop F_1 will be transferred to flipflop F_2 by pulling down on the cathode of gate G. This

transfer is independent of the states of F_1 and F_2.

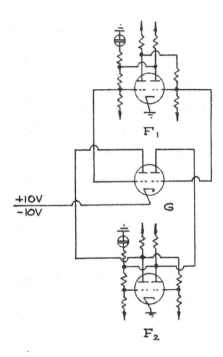

Double Gating a Flipflop

Figure 2.6

In other words, the flipflop is gated only with the combination of
zero volts on the grid and -10 volts on the cathode of the gate tube.

Balancing of Gates. As has been previously discussed, a gate of the single tube type can, if preceded by an appropriate clear action, change a flipflop to "0" or to "1". If the flipflop were cleared to zero, the gate tube would be connected to pin 1 of the flipflop. Otherwise it would be connected to pin 0. Inevitably the gate tube will place a capacitive load on the flipflop plate, slowing the transient action of the flipflop. In order to minimize this loading effect paralleling of gates is avoided and whenever possible the gates are placed on the flipflop in a balanced manner. In the ORDVAC registers this amounts to connecting one and only one gate to a flipflop plate.

Since each ORDVAC double-register consists of two single registers, two flipflops per column are available. This means that four gates per double register are the maximum that can be used if the principles discussed above are to be followed. Further, two sets of gates are restricted to one single register and the other to the second register. It will be shown later that the two double registers (or "shifting registers") require three gates per double-register, leaving one gate for other purposes. It will also be shown that this fourth gate is used for an entrance gate from the adder for one case and from the memory in the other case.

THE R_I REGISTER. (Drawing 359). This double register is made up of two rows of 40 flipflops and of four sets of gates. The upper row of flipflops is called R^1 while the lower row is called R_1 and is the accumulator. Only three of the four sets of gates are used for gating, and a few tubes of the fourth set have been used for control

purposes. This is described under Multiplication Roundoff.

The three sets of gates which are used are given in Table 2.1.

These gates are used for shifting words in R_I.

GATE	FUNCTION
Yellow Gate R^1 (YGR^1)	Transfers straight up from R_1 to R^1
Black Gate R_1 (BGR$_1$)	Transfers down right from R^1 to R_1
Red Gate R_1 (RGR$_1$)	Transfers down left from R^1 to R_1.

Table 2.1

Gating in R_I

There is a fourth gate, mounted on a separate chassis above

R_I, which is used to transfer words from the adder into R^1. This is

Green gate R^1. (GGR^1). The unused R_I gate also has the name GGR^1, but

since it is never used for gating purposes there is no confusion.

Because of the one-sided character of the gates, it is necess-

ary to be able to clear R^1 and R_2. And, since the gates are balanced,

two of the clears are to 1 and two are to 0. Each gate must be pre-

ceded by its appropriate clear. If the clear is to 0, the gate trans-

fers 1's, if the clear is to 1, the gate transfers 0's. Table 2.2

lists the clears and gates and their properties.

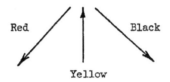

Figure 2.6a
Gate Coding

53

CLEAR			ACTION	GATE	ACTION
Red Clear	R^1	(RCR^1)	R^1 to 1's	GGR^1	Gates 0's from adder
Black Clear	R^1	(BCR^1)	R^1 to 0's	YGR^1	Gates 1's from R_1
Yellow Clear	R_1	(YCR_1)	R_1 to 0's	BGR_1	Gates 1's from R^1
Green Clear	R_1	(GCR_1)	R_1 to 1's	RGR_1	Gates 0's from R^1

Table 2.2

Gates and Clears in R_I

The gates and clears always occur in pairs, the combinations being RC-GG, BC-YG, YC-BG, GC-RG.

R_1, THE ACCUMULATOR. This register has other connections besides those given above:

(1) It receives input words from the input tape (See Chapter 3);

(2) It connects to the memory so that its contents may be transferred into the memory. (See Chapter 4). All information going to the memory must pass through R_1;

(3) It connects to the adder; (See Section 2.7 of this Chapter);

(4) It connects with R_2 by shifting. (See Section 2.6).

The accumulator plays a very important role in all of the machine operations. It holds the operands dividend, augend and sub-trahend and receives the sum as well as the sign and most significant 39 digits of a product. It is the only register from which words may be transferred to the memory, and it receives serially from the right-hand end each word of a tape as it is read into the machine.

54

There are two gates into R_1: RGR_1 and BGR_1; there is one gate out of R_1: YGR^1. The transfer to the memory is not a gate in the ordinary sense and is discussed in Chapter 4. The transfer to the adder is not a gate.

R^1 REGISTER. This register is used for holding numbers temporarily. There are two gates into it: YGR^1 and GGR^1, the former from R_1 and the latter from the digit resolver. There are two gates out of it: RGR_1 and BGR_1.

2.4 THE R_{II} REGISTER. (Drawing 360). This double register is similar in construction to R_I and has two parts, R_2 and R^2. The register R_2 is also called the arithmetic register.

All four of the sets of gates in R_{II} are utilized, although only three are needed for internal transfers within R_{II}. The fourth gate is used to transfer from the memory to R_2 in the execution of the R order. The gates are given in Table 2.3.

GATE		FUNCTION
Yellow Gate R^2	(YGR^2)	Transfers straight up from R_2 to R^2
Black Gate R_2	(BGR_2)	Transfers down right from R^2 to R_2
Red Gate R_2	(RGR_2)	Transfers down left from R^2 to R_2
Green Gate R_2	(GGR_2)	Transfers from memory to R_2

Table 2.3. Gating in R_{II}.

The clears in R_{II} are similar to those in R_I except that no RCR^2 is needed, there being no necessity to clear R^2 to 1's. The clears and gates for R_{II} are given in Table 2.4:

CLEAR	ACTION	GATE	ACTION
Black Clear R^2 (BCR^2)	R^2 to 0's	YGR^2	Gates 1's from R_2.
Yellow Clear R_2 (YCR_2)	R_2 to 0's	BGR_2	Gates 1's from R^2.
Green Clear R_2 (GCR_2)	R_2 to 1's	RGR_2	Gates 0's from R^2.
		GGR_2	Gates 0's from memory.

Table 2.4

Gates and Clears in R_{II}

R_2, The Arithmetic Register. The arithmetic register holds the multiplier and receives the quotient. There are three gates into it, as shown in Table 2.4, and two gates out of it. One of these is YGR^2. The other is a gate to R^3 called YGR^3 using gate tubes in R_{III}. This gate is used in the A orders.

R^2 Register. This register holds numbers temporarily. There is one gate into it: YGR^2; there are two gates from it: BGR_2 and RGR_2.

2.5 THE R_{III} REGISTER. (Drawing 361). This register, built like R_I and R_{II} for convenience, is wired differently and is actually two completely independent registers, R^3 the number register and R_3 the order register. The order register is a part of the control, being the recipient of order pairs as they come from the memory, and is

56

discussed in Chapter 5, but it will be discussed here also for the sake of completeness. Three of the four R_{III} gates are used.

R^3, The Number Register. This register is the chief entry from the memory into the arithmetic unit, receiving addend, multiplicand and divisor. The gate used is GGR^3, which is preceded by RCR^3 and gates 0's from the memory. There is also YGR^3, preceded by BCR^3, which gates 1's from R_2 as mentioned in Section 2.4.

The only exit from R^3 is to the complement gate (Section 2.9) which in turn communicates with the adder.

R_3, The Order Register. Each order pair comes to R_3 from the memory, being transferred by RGR_3 after GCR_3. There are three sets of gates associated with R_3: (1) the even order gate,

            (2) the odd order gate,

            (3) the odd address gate.

The functions of these gates are fully discussed in Part II of Chapter 5. The first two transfer orders to the decoding register and the second moves the odd address to the even address location.

There are also connections going from the even address location of R_3 to the following places:

            (1) the control counter,

            (2) the address generator,

            (3) the recognition circuit.

The gating from R_3 is shown in Drawing 266. Table 2.5 gives the clears and gates for R_{III}.

CLEAR	ACTION	GATE	ACTION
BCR^3	R^3 to 0's	YGR^3	Gates 1's from R_2
RCR^3	R^3 to 1's	GGR^3	Gates 0's from memory
GCR_3	R_3 to 1's	RGR_3	Gates 0's from memory

TABLE 2.5

Gates and Clears in R_{III}

2.6 REGISTER SHIFTING AND INTERCONNECTION. The registers R_I and R_{II} are shifting registers whose contents are shifted under the direction of the control by appropriate sequencing of the clears and gates. The R_{II} register is a slave of R_I, and no shift in R_I can be made without causing a corresponding shift in R_{II}. Thus in multiplication as the product forms in R_I with right shifts, R_2 is shifted for inspection of the multiplier digit. Similarly, in division as R_1 goes left so does R_2, permitting the digitwise insertion of the quotient. The shifting of contents of registers is described in Section 5.2.

2.7 <u>THE ADDER</u>. (Drawing 104). The adder is a component of the addition unit. The addition unit, consisting of the adder and digit resolver, performs addition in parallel and is an analog device; i.e., the necessary logical operations needed for addition are simulated by adding analogous currents and measuring the voltage across a resistor.

The function of the adder is to simulate for each column being added the result of adding three binary digits: the resident digit (augend), the incident digit (addend), and a carry digit which is received from the column to the right. The eight input possibilities for each column are as follows:

Resident Digit	0 0 1 1 0 0 1 1
Incident Digit	0 1 0 1 0 1 0 1
Carry Digit from right	0 0 0 0 1 1 1 1

The four output possibilities are as follows:

Sum Digit	0 0 1 1
Carry to Left Digit	0 1 0 1

The adder establishes four levels of voltage corresponding to 00, 01, 10, 11 (i.e., to 0, 1, 2, and 3 in decimal notation). It also establishes a carry voltage for 10 or 11 and feeds this to the next most significant stage.

Operation of the Adder. Figure 2.7 shows one stage of the adder. The three inputs to any stage are to tubes A, B and C. The plate voltage S of A and B represents the sum, which can be one of four values. The tubes A and B can each allow 4.85 ma to pass through the 10.3K resistor, depending upon the addend and augend. The voltage supplied to the 10.3K resistor will be either 160 or 210 v, depending upon the carry from the preceding stage. We thus have the following possibilities.

ADDEND	AUGEND	CARRY	SUM	CURRENT IN 10.3K RESISTOR	VOLTAGE AT SUMMING POINT
0	0	0	0	.. 0.6 ma	204v
0	0	1	1	0.6	154
0	1	0	1	5.45	154
0	1	1	10	5.45	104
1	0	0	1	5.45	154
1	0	1	10	5.45	104
1	1	0	10	10.30	104
1	1	1	11	10.30	54

Table 2.6

Adder Voltages at the Summing
Point

Two uses are made of the sum voltage. On the one hand, it goes to the digit resolver. On the other a carry voltage for the next stage must be produced. This carry voltage is obtained by differentiating at the 115V level between the cases 0, 1 and the cases

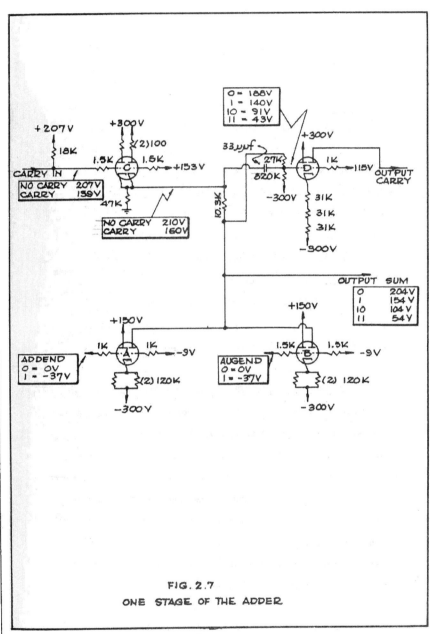

FIG. 2.7

ONE STAGE OF THE ADDER

61

2, 3 with tube D.

Forty Stage Adder. Drawing 104 gives the circuit diagram
of the adder. The sense of the columns as shown is opposite to the
sense of the registers, the least significant binary digit being in
Column 2 of the adder circuit diagram and carry propagation being
to the right on the diagram. This is because the adder is mounted
with its back to the connecting registers. The resident digit
constant current gates are those tubes in row 2. The incident digit
constant current gates are in row 3 and odd columns. The carry
selection gates are in row 1 and row 4. The capacitor shown between
the carry input and the input to the carry gate is for the purpose
of speeding up the production of the carry voltage. Two tubes are
used for a carry into the least significant stage. These are discussed in Section 2.9 and under addition and subtraction in Section
5.9.

2.8 THE DIGIT RESOLVER. (drawing 200). The adder produces
a sum digit and a carry digit for each column. The sum digit is 0
if the sum is 00 or 10 and it is 1 if the sum is 01 or 11. That is,
if the adder voltage is 204v or 104v the sum digit is 0 while if it
is 154v or 54v the sum digit is 1. These cases must be distinguished.

The entire set of 40 sum digits constitutes the desired output of the addition unit. The resolving of the sum into a sum digit
is achieved by selective constant current gates which open and close
at various points in the range of voltage levels representing the
sum. Referring to drawing 200 we see that the selective action is as

62

follows. Noting that the three gates draw current from a common point, each drawing 1.77 milliamperes, we have the results shown in Table 2.7.

SUM	SUM VOLTAGE	ROW 2 GATE	ROW 4 GATE	ROW 6 GATE	TOTAL CURRENT
00	204V	Off	On	Off	1.77 ma
01	154	On	On	Off	3.54
10	104	On	Off	Off	1.77
11	54	On	Off	On	3.54

Table 2.7

Digit Resolver Characteristics

The total current is drawn through a 56K resistor from +150V. The output voltage is given by Table 2.8.

SUM	SUM DIGIT	OUTPUT VOLTAGE
00	0	+51V
01	1	-49
10	0	+51
11	1	-49

Table 2.8

Digit Resolver Output Voltages

Hence +51V correspond to a 0 sum digit and -49V to a 1.

The output of the digit resolver is connected to GGR[1]

(drawing 127). Actually, as can be seen, the digit resolver output is prevented from rising above OV so that $0 = 0$ volts and $1 = -49$ volts. The pegging is done by diodes in the gate chassis.

2.9 THE COMPLEMENT GATE. (Drawing 155). The complement gate provides the equivalent of subtraction as discussed in Section 1.4. The complement gate in reality consists of two gates. The input to one gate comes from number 5 grid on the R_3 flipflop and the other input is from number 6 grid. The outputs of the two gates are in parallel (by common cathodes) and a means is provided for selecting one and only one gate at a given time by controlling the plate supply voltages to the gates.

In order to form a complete complement it is necessary to add 1 in the least significant place (Section 1.3) after having complemented each digit. This is the end around carry and is done by using the otherwise unused carry into the least significant stage of the adder. Whenever the complement gate is set to the subtract state the #3 grid on the tube in Row 4, Column 1 of the adder (Drawing 104) goes negative and causes a carry voltage to be present at pin 2 of the tube in Row 4 of the first stage. This is equivalent to adding 2^{-39}.

It was mentioned in Section 2.1 that ordinarily the #5 grid is sensed to determine the state of the flipflop with $-37V = 1$ and $OV = 0$. It is evident that if the number 6 grid were sensed instead, the resultant effect would be the exact equivalent of complementing the state of each flipflop as far as the nature of the information obtained

64

is concerned. Therefore, when the number 2 plates of the complement gate tubes are high with +90V and the number 1 plates are low with -30V, the number 5 grid of the register flipflop is sensed. This represents the non-complement state. When the number 1 plate is high and the number 2 plate is low the number 6 grid of the toggle is sensed, representing the complemented state.

2.10 **GATE AND CLEAR DRIVERS** . The units which furnish the voltages for the various gates and clears are discussed in this ·section. These units get their signals from the control, the signals originating in the shift sequencing chassis.

Register Gate Drivers. (Drawings 201, 202, 280). Each gate driver consists of a 5687 cathode follower operating at 10 milliamperes and another 5687 acting as a clamp to prevent the negative swing of the output from exceeding about -14V. The gate driver feeds a set of cathode followers in the registers which in turn drive the gate cathodes. There are 4 gate drivers for R_I, 3 for R_{II} and 3 for R_{III}.

Register Clear Drivers . (Drawing 130). Each register clear driver consists of 12 parallel 5687 triode sections which drive the register plate bus as a cathode load. One clear driver thus furnishes the plate currentfor one side of the 40 flipflops in a register. There are 4 clear drivers for R_I, 3 for R_{II} and 3 for R_{III}.

65

Complement Gate Driver. (Drawing 198). The complement
gate driver consists of two units, each the same as the drawing except for the bleeder on the input. This holds the complement
gate in the add state if there is no input. Each unit takes the
control signal for complement or non-complement, which is a "push-
pull" signal 0V and -20V, and generates a complement or non-complement
signal +90V and -30V for input to the complement gate. The output
consists of four 5687 triode sections in parallel.

CHAPTER 3

THE INPUT-OUTPUT

The input-output equipment consists of teletypewriter units together with those circuits of the computer used in performing the two orders: input 80028, and print, 80828.

The input order takes 40 binary digits from 10 successive rows of a tape that has been previously punched with 4 binary digits per row, and puts them in order in R_1. It does this by successively shifting left and gating into the four right hand digits of R_1.

The print order prints one word on a sheet of paper as ten sexadecimal digits. These are formed by taking the 40 binary digits in R_2 four at a time, beginning with the sign digit, and printing a corresponding base 16 symbol.

3.1 PUNCHED TAPE. The paper tape used is standard five hole teletypewriter tape, 11/16 of an inch wide. Four of the five holes are used to represent sexadecimal digits in a binary code. All five holes are punched to serve as a space between words. There is also a smaller row of holes in the center of the tape that fits the feed sprocket that moves the tape. The appearance of a tape punched with each of the binary codes and the corresponding sexadecimal symbols is shown in Drawing 355.

3.2 THE INPUT TRANSMITTER-DISTRIBUTOR. A transmitter-distributor is used to sense the holes in the tape. The wiring of a standard unit has been modified as shown in Drawing 174. The punched tape passes over pins in the transmitter. At appropriate times these pins are raised against the tape. If there is a hole above a tape pin, the pin will move farther than if there is no hole. This difference in amount of travel is used to position a single-pole double-throw switch associated with each of the five tape pins. The setting of these switches at the time that the pins are raised corresponds to the binary code punched in that row of.holes in the tape. The distributor consists of a commutator with seven segments and a brush connected mechanically to the same shaft that raises and lowers the tape pins and advances the tape. The brush makes one revolution for each row of holes in the tape. The seven segments are known as the stop segment, the start segment, and segments 1 through 5.

When the transmitter-distributor is at rest, the brush rests upon the stop segment, the tape pins are retracted, and one row of holes on the tape is over the tape pins. When the clutch release magnet is energized, the main shaft begins to turn. While the brush is passing over the remainder of the stop segment and the start segment, the tape is advanced one row of holes and the tape pins are raised. The tape pins and tape now remain stationary while the brush passes over segments 1 through 5. When it again reaches the stop segment, the tape pins are retracted and the transmitter-distributor is ready to read the next row of holes. Once

68

the shaft has started rotating, de-energizing the clutch release magnet will not stop the shaft until the next time the brush gets to the stop segment and the pins are retracted.

3.3 THE INPUT CIRCUIT. The operation of the input circuit can be followed on Drawing 356. Digits are gated into R_1 by means of gate tubes connected to the plates of the flipflops 2^{-36}, 2^{-37}, 2^{-38}, and $2^{-39}R_1$. Single gating is used and 1's are gated. The voltage at the grids of the gate tubes is determined by the setting of the single-pole double-throw switches associated with the four tape pins that read the binary positions on the tape.

The input operation begins when the two signals (go enable) and (input and operate) cause the input start relay to be de-energized. The contacts of this relay open the holding circuit to the tape stop relay coil. When the tape stop relay releases, one of its sets of contacts energizes the clutch release magnet of the transmitter-distributor and the brush starts to leave its rest position on the stop segment.

Nothing further happens until the brush reaches the beginning of segment 1 and operates the shift relay. When the shift relay is energized, it sets a flipflop to "1". The state of this flipflop is compared with the first stage of the shift counter. If the states disagree, a black clear is enabled which is the first step of a left shift. During the first left shift the shift counter counts to one and so the state of the first stage no longer agrees with the state of the flipflop in the input-output circuit. This

69

disables the black clear and prevents another left shift from
taking place. After about 20 milliseconds the brush leaves segment 1 and the shift relay is de-energized, resetting the flipflop to "0". The flipflop and the first stage of the shift counter
again agree and so a second left shift is enabled. The same cycle
takes place as the brush passes over segments 3 and 4, which produce a total of four left shifts.

When the brush reaches segment 5, it lowers the voltage
on the grid of a cathode follower. The output of the cathode follower is connected to the cathodes of the four gate tubes to R_1. Thus,
the gate tubes are enabled and gate four binary digits from the tape
to R_1.

When the brush again reaches the stop segment, one revolution of the brush shaft has been completed. On the second revolution, the tape is advanced, four more left shifts are made, and
the next four binary digits are gated.

This cycle of shifting and gating is repeated eight more
times to gate in the rest of the 40 binary digits. Near the end
of the tenth revolution, when the brush leaves segment 3, the
fortieth left shift is performed. The shift counter is then at
40 which agrees with the number in the address part of the tape
order. The recognition circuit sends out a recognize signal. When
the brush passes over segment 4 and reaches segment 5, the last four
digits are gated into R_1.

As the brush passes over the stop and start segments on
the eleventh revolution, the tape pins sense the eleventh row of

70

holes in the tape. If the tape was correctly prepared, this row
of holes will contain the space code. The switch that is associated
with tape pin number 1, which never senses a hole for any of the
sexadecimal codes, will now move to the "hole" state and energize
the tape stop relay. The tape stop relay has three sets of contacts.
One removes the ground from the distributor brush so that the shift
relay will not be operated on this revolution and also closes a
holding circuit for the tape stop relay. The second opens the circuit to the gate cathode follower grid. The third de-energizes the
clutch release magnet so that the brush will stop at the end of the
eleventh revolution. A cathode follower that is fastened to the
clutch release magnet sends a negative tape end signal to the interplay control, and the computer is ready to proceed with the next
order.

   3.4 THE OUTPUT OPERATION. The output circuit forms the
usual type of time sequence signal for the operation of either a
teletypewriter or a nontyping reperforator. This consists of seven
parts: stop, start and five digit times. Each portion of the signal is about 20 milliseconds in duration. During the stop portion
of the signal, and also whenever the circuit is at rest, the circuit
to the printer line magnet is closed. During the start time the
circuit is opened. The start signal sets the printer mechanism
in operation. During the remaining five signal times the circuit
to the printer line magnet may be either opened or closed depending
upon the particular five digit code that is being sent to the printer.

The standard teletype code uses five digits to give 2^5 characters. The binary code that is used with ORDVAC, however, uses only 4 digits to give 16 characters plus an extra code of all five "1"'s for a space. The four digits that are used are numbers 2 through 5 in the time sequence.

The operation of the output circuit may be followed by referring to Drawing 356.

The signal for the printer line is timed by a modified transmitter-distributor. Only the distributor portion is used. The output circuit senses the digit in $2^0 R_2$. The word in R_2 is shifted left one digit at a time under the control of the output transmitter-distributor until all 40 digits have been sensed and printed as 10 sexadecimal characters.

In its rest position on the stop segment, the brush keeps the stop relay energized. This relay supplies the stop signal to the printer line. A second set of contacts on this relay is connected to the stepping relay magnet. This stepping relay has 11 positions and is of the cyclic type, i.e., it moves from position 11 back to position 1. The stepping relay is cocked when its magnet coil is energized. When the circuit to the magnet coil is broken, a spring causes the relay to move to the next position. At the beginning of the output operation the stepping relay is in position 11.

The output operation begins when the two signals (output and operate) and (go enable) cause the output start relay to release. This energizes the clutch release magnet and the brush begins to move. The output relay also closes the circuit to the stepping relay magnet through the contacts of the stop relay which was already operated. This cocks the stepping relay which is still in position 11.

When the brush moves to the start segment the start relay is operated and sends the start signal to the printer line. The stop relay is de-energized and in turn de-energizes the magnet of the stepping relay. The stepping relay then moves to position 1.

As the brush moves to segment 1 of the distributor, the 1 relay is operated. This opens the printer line circuit regardless of the state of the digit relay and sends a "0" or "no hole" signal to the printer.

The digit relay is connected to the flipflop $2^0 R_2$. If the digit in this flipflop is a "1", the digit relay is energized; if the digit is a "0", the digit relay is not energized. This will cause the circuit to the printer line magnet to be either closed or opened, respectively, during the time the brush is on segment 2.

When the brush first hits segment 3, the shift relay is energized. This enables exactly one left shift by the same means that was described in section 4.1. The second digit of the word that is to be printed is now in the flipflop $2^0 R_2$, and the digit relay is operated or not according to its value. The second digit of the word then determines whether or not the circuit to the printer line magnet is opened or closed during the time the brush is on

73

segment 3.

As the brush leaves segment 3, the shift relay is de-energized and a second left shift is enabled. The third digit of the word in R_2 is now sent to the printer line during the time the brush is on segment 4.

When the brush reaches segment 5, the shift relay is energized and another left shift is enabled. This causes the fourth digit of the word to determine whether the line to the printer magnet is opened or closed. A fourth shift is enabled when the brush leaves segment 5 and the shift relay releases.

When the brush reaches the stop segment at the completion of its first revolution, the stop signal is again sent to the printer. The signals that have been sent to the printer will cause one base sixteen character to be printed corresponding to the first four binary digits of the word that was in R_2. The stepping relay is cocked and ready to step to position 2, as soon as the brush leaves the stop segment and releases the stop relay.

As the brush passes over the start segment and segment 1, two open circuits are sent to the printer. During the remainder of the second revolution of the brush, signals corresponding to the digits 4 through 7 of the word in R_2 are sent to the printer. These signals cause a second sexadecimal character to be selected in the printer.

Revolutions three through nine of the brush send 28 more binary digits to the printers in groups of four.

As the brush leaves segment 5 near the completion of the tenth revolution, the fortieth left shift is enabled. The digit that was originally in $2^{-39}R_2$ now gets shifted off the end. At this point the contents of the shift counter agree with the address in the output order and so the recognition circuit produces a recognize output. An end signal is then sent from the arithmetic stop chassis to the interplay control and the computer goes on to the next order. Part of the output circuit continues to function, however. The brush makes an 11th revolution. As it hits the stop segment, the stepping relay is cocked to step to position 11 and the stop signal is sent to the printer line. As the brush passes over the start segment, the start signal is sent to the printer line and the stepping relay moves to position 11. When the relay is in position 11 it keeps the circuit to the printer line magnet closed as the brush passes over the five digit segments. This sends a "five holes" or "space" signal to the printer. It also opens the circuit to the clutch release magnet which had been held closed in position 1 through 10. The distributor shaft will therefore stop at the end of the 11th revolution unless at that time there is another output order in R_3. While the stepping relay is in the 11th position, the circuit to the shift relay is opened to prevent unwanted left shifts should another output order come along while the space signal was still being sent.

CHAPTER 4

THE MEMORY

The general requirements for a memory are that it be
possible to write information into it, read information from it,
and store the information. The memory used in ORDVAC is of the
Williams type in which information is stored as a potential distribution on the phosphor surface of a cathode ray tube.

A brief description of the fundamental process of this
storage system can be given for a single address or spot of the
cathode ray tube. If we consider a beam of electrons falling on
this spot, then for most "ordinary" potentials of the phosphor the
secondary electron emission ratio is greater than one, so that when
a beam of electrons initially strikes the phosphor, the number of
electrons which leaves the phosphor is greater than the number received by the phosphor. In a very short time the spot in question
becomes more positive in potential with respect to any point of
fixed potential, and it continues to change in potential until it
becomes sufficiently positive to reduce the number of electrons
which leave that spot. Eventually, an equiblibrium is reached when
the number of electrons arriving equals the number of electrons
leaving but at this time the region is positive with respect to the
surrounding phosphor. Since the phosphor and the glass are very
good insulators, this potential distribution is retained for a few
tenths of a second without noticeable change. In order to make a
storage system, it is necessary to sense the existence or non-existence
of the potential distribution which has just been described. In the
terminology which follows, if the beam is turned on at a single spot
and turned off according to the foregoing description, the spot in

76

question is called a dot and represents the binary digit 1 in ORDVAC. The potential distribution corresponding to a dot can be altered, and in fact, "destroyed" by turning on the beam at a location immediately adjacent to the original position. When this is done in the ORDVAC memory the resulting potential distribution for the dot is called a dash and represents the binary digit 0.

It is possible at a later time to detect the difference between the two potential distributions just described by turning on the beam at the original dot position. If this is done and the previous potential distribution corresponds to that of a dot (or 1), then the potential distribution on the phosphor will already have been in existence and no displacement current will be registered by a screen placed on the outside surface of the cathode ray tube. But if the potential distribution were that corresponding to a dash, the potential at the dot position would have been "destroyed" and the process of turning on the beam would recreate the dot potential and a displacement current would be sensed by the screen attached to the cathode ray tube. Thus by this simple explanation the detection screen would sense a positive signal if the previous distribution had been that of a dash, and the sensing screen would detect no signal if the previous distribution had been that of a dot. This explanation must be altered somewhat because of the field produced by the existence of the electrons in the electron beam. This field tends to make both the dot signal and the dash signal as observed on the pick-up screen somewhat more negative than would otherwise be the case so that the resulting signals are negative for a dot (or 1) and positive for a dash (or 0). This explanation is a brief one which may be helpful in understanding the following pages, but it should be understood that it may not be physically precise.

Storage of information on the phosphor must be accomplished for periods

77

much longer than 1/10 of a second, which is the longest safe time
permitted on the cathode ray tube surface. This storage is accomplished
by "regeneration". In the ORDVAC memory facilities are provided so that
when the memory is not in use for arithmetic operations a test is made
of each spot of the memory in order and each spot is regenerated by
appropriately turning on or off the beam so that a "fair" dot is regenerated into a "good" dot and a "fair" dash is regenerated into a
"good" dash. By this scheme, it is possible to hold information in the
memory for indefinite periods of time. The relationship of the dot
and dash spot is shown in Figure 4.1.

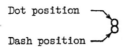

Dot position

Dash position

Figure 4.1   Spot Relationship

4.1 <u>GENERAL OPERATION AND LOGICAL STRUCTURE</u>. The ORDVAC
memory operates in two separate phases: an <u>action</u> cycle and a <u>regenerate</u>
cycle. The first is the sequence of operations which must be carried
out to write into or read from the memory. The second is the sequence
of operations which must be carried out to refresh the contents of the
memory and prevent their being lost. A regeneration process is always
going on whenever the memory is not being written into or read from -
as, for example, while the arithmetic for a multiplication is being
done. Drawing 350 indicates how the various elements of the memory
are arranged. The primary driving unit for the regeneration system is
the memory clock. It is used to trigger a pulser chain which directly

78

controls the various operations the memory performs in storage. Pulses from
the pulsers drive a dispatch counter (Section 5.16) which is used to provide
information about where the beam will be positioned during regeneration and
during the reading out of orders from the memory. These pulses are also used
in the memory synchronization chassis for tying the memory to the remainder
of the machine. In the regeneration chassis, they, along with signals picked
up from the cathode ray tube screen, are combined logically to provide regeneration of the raster and for reading into and out of the memory. The
address generator decodes the information in the address part of an order and
in the control counter and positions the beams of all 40 cathode ray tubes in
parallel along with a slave used to view the contents of the memory.

Drawing 333 indicates the pulse chain which is generated upon the
advent of one clock pulse. The clock delivers one pulse every 24 microseconds.
The operation which ensues is dependent upon the signals which have been designated as "A" and "R" on Drawing 196. Actually, the "A" signal indicates
to the regeneration chassis that information is to be written into the memory.
The "R" signal means that a regeneration is to be performed or information
is to be read out of the memory. These are identical operations so far as
the memory is concerned.

The operations performed by the regeneration chassis are indicated
by the logical diagram in Drawing 351. Since the operations "A" and "R"
are complementary, one of them may be considered to be on during any regeneration or write-in cycle.

Let it be assumed that the signals on the action and
regenerate wires indicate regenerate. Then, upon the advent of a

79

dot pulse, the beam will be turned on at a position already set
by the address generator.   The beam will bombard the spot in
question and a characteristic signal will be coupled to the pick-
up screen depending upon whether a charge did or did not reside
at the spot. The signals are similar to those shown in Figure
4.2.

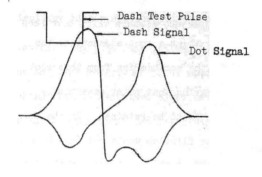

Figure 4.2

Memory Signals

These signals are those coming from the amplifier and, as the amplifier used is rather nonlinear, they probably bear only polarity similarity to the actual signals at the screen. At the output of the amplifier the signals are presented to a gate controlled by the dash test pulse. Its relative position and time phase is shown in Figure 4.2. Signals rising above the dash test pulse open the gate to set the flipflop. The "or" circuit preceding the gate is merely a clamp to limit the positive excursion of the dash signal presented to the gate.

After the setting of the flipflop (if there is a dash signal) an additional "and" circuit is activated which leaves the beam turned on. The regenerate dash pulse, however, sets a flipflop (not shown here) which causes the address generator to insert a slight vertical motion to the beam, thus positioning it at a spot adjacent to the original one. While turned on here the secondaries from this spot discharge the original spot, thus leaving that point essentially uncharged, as it should be if a dash is to be retained. If the sensed spot had been a charged one, then the flipflop would not have been set and the beam would have turned off at the completion of the dot signal prior to the incremental vertical motion and the charged would have been maintained at the original spot.

In order to read out the information in the memory, it is but necessary to look at the signal from the cathode follower on the 0 side of the flipflop.

If the input to the regeneration chassis is action, then
the beam will still turn on with the advent of a dot pulse. The
sensing process will be the same even to the turning over of the
flipflop. This information is not used in the operation but is
merely done for uniformity of circuitry considerations. The beam
will stay on after the dot pulse goes off due to the presence of
the writing dash pulse if the digit to be read in from the accumulator is a 0. The address generator will again reposition the spot
slightly with the start of the regeneration dash and so a dash will
be written in. If the incoming digit is a 1, it will be turned off
at the completion of the dot pulse. Thus an uncharged spot or a
dash corresponds to a 0 and a charged spot or a dot to a 1.

4.2 CIRCUITS.

Video Amplifier and Williams Tube Control. (Drawing 196)
This is the basic chassis. This chassis contains the amplifier and
logical circuitry associated with the beam control.

Each chassis (of which there are 40) is mounted above its
cathode ray tube, and the power and driving pulses enter and leave
through a 16-pin socket in the end of the chassis. Drawing 358
shows the physical layout of the tubes, the plug connections, and
the output and input lugs other than these. The pickup screen from
the face of the cathode ray tube is connected to the input of the
amplifier by a lead passed through a piece of braid and down through
a hole in the top of the cathode ray tube shield. The braid is
soldered to the wall inside the tube shield. The fore end of the

chassis is bolted to the tube shield with a screw turned into a tapped hole in the chassis. When the chassis is in operating condition, a phosphor bronze lead is soldered to lug No. 4 on the front of the chassis and goes to the grid of the corresponding flipflop in the accumulator register. Lug 3 is the output lead and passes down an insulated wire to a terminal board and then through phosphor·bronze leads to the order, arithmetic, and memory registers.

It will be found that this chassis will require repairs more than any other in the machine, both because of the number involved and because due to the high amplifier gain, it is the most sensitive. These repairs will be discussed later.

In normal operation the output from this chassis will be used to adjust the memory for focus, intensity and astigmatism. Lug number 1 on the chassis front is generally used to observe the amplifier output. It is connected to the cathode of the last amplifier stage through a 1K resistor. Signals here are about 0.5 volts in amplitude, and the amplifier output signals as shown in Figure 4.3 are present.

Address Generator. (Drawing 195). The address generator positions the beam on the tubes and drives all deflection plates in parallel. The positioning information is delivered in two sets to two inputs of the address generator, one from the order register, digits 2^{-10} through 2^{-19}, and the other from the common side of the dispatch counter. These are supplied to the deflection circuits in

accordance with signals from the memory synchronization chassis,
the inputs coming from the order register on the action signal
and from the dispatch counter on regenerate. The logical circuitry
involved in this process is indicated in Figure 4.3.

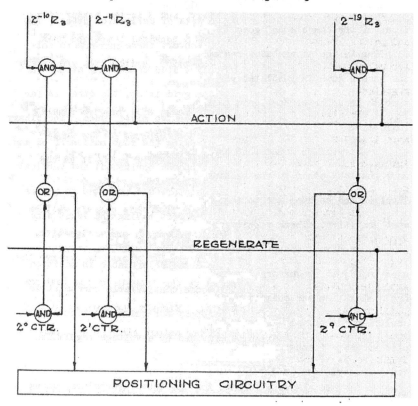

Figure 4.3 Beam Positioning
Circuitry

It should be noted that the <u>ACTION</u> signal here is not identical
to the one called A in the video amplifier and Williams tube control chassis. As noted, that one appears only upon writing into the

memory. This action signal appears whenever information is to be read into or out of an address specified by the order register.

The binary information is converted into voltages by the tubes in row 5, columns 2 through 11. These tubes act as constant current sources pulling on the two sets of deflection buses. The common plate resistors are used to convert these currents to voltages. Each of these tubes has only 1 side conducting at any one time during its use, and so when one grid is up, the other is far down. This yields the push-pull on the two plate buses. The binary information is moved in steps by altering the combination of on and off sides of the five tubes in each of the horizontal and vertical deflection systems. The cathode resistors are arranged in powers of two, those tubes having the most effect having the least size cathode resistors.

As the deflections must be absolutely stable in position from one regeneration to another, some considerable care must be exercised in regulating the -150 supply for the deflection cathode resistors. This regulation is provided by a voltage regulation circuit of fairly long time constant.

The plate supply voltage for the tubes determines, along with the total deflections, the average value of the push-pull voltages to the deflection plates. In order to have proper astigmatism adjustment of the cathode ray tube one must be sure that the average values of the vertical and horizontal voltages are the same. Since the raster is square and the vertical deflection sensitivity is less than the horizontal, larger voltages are needed for the vertical deflection. This means that the positive supply voltage for the vertical deflection resistors must be somewhat higher. The cathode follower source for this side is then correspondingly higher.

In order to keep external noises coming from the cathode ray tubes from disturbing the deflection lines, the 40 tubes are split into two groups of 20 and these are driven so that the deflections are reversed. This tends to cancel out noises coupled to the deflection plates which would have a push pull component due to the differences in capacity of the two plates of each set.

Twitch Chassis. (Drawing 318). In order to gain a reasonably good space factor between spots, the raster has been adjusted so that nearly equilateral triangles are formed. This means that each address is surrounded by six other addresses on the corners of a hexagon, as shown in Figure 4.4.

Figure 4.4. Raster Pattern

86

The twitch chassis shown in Drawing 318 does this by shifting every other row a half address horizontally as dictated by the first vertical stage of the address generator. The twitch is vertical. It was found that by reversing the direction of the twitch on every other row a better spacing could be achieved for an improvement of the read-around ratio. (See Section 4.3). The read-around ratio was optimized by adjusting the unit vertical spacing in the address generator such that all six surrounding spots failed at the same read-around ratio.

Diode Chassis.(Drawing 231). Noises which come into the address generator from the counter and order register are clipped off on the upper end by the grid circuit of the inverter tubes in Row 4 of the address generator. To clip off noise on the lower edge a diode, returned to a low impedance source of -14 volts, is fastened on the input grid of this inverter. The circuit of these tubes is shown in Drawing 231.

Clock.(Drawing 370). The primary driving source for the memory system is the clock shown in Drawing 370. This circuit produces a sharp positive spike every 24 microseconds to trigger the differentiating networks into the pulsers.

Pulsers, (Drawing 318). The standard memory pulser is shown in Drawing 368. There are eight of these pulsers mounted in pairs. The lengths of the pulses may be adjusted by altering the resistor R. The positive limit for the pulses is set by resistor R_1, the negative by resistor R_2. These values differ from chassis to chassis somewhat due to the difference in pulse lengths and the cathode follower banks used with some of the pulses.

Pulser Cathode Followers . (Drawing 176). This chassis provides the driving power for some of the pulses to the memory which require either more current or speed than the output cathode follower of the pulser is capable of supplying. Drawing 176 shows the distribution of the cathode followers to the pulses.

Bleeder Chain and Connections . (Drawing 216). Drawing 216 gives the bleeder chain which supplies the electrodes. The focus and intensity potentiometers are mounted above the memory positions on the front of the tube; the astigmatism potentiometers are mounted at the rear and are adjusted from the front with a shaft which comes through the tube shield cover. The bypass condensers are placed to the rear of each cathode ray tube socket as are the diodes.

The astigmatism control driver attached at X is shown separately at the top of the drawing.

Slave Tube and Associated Circuitry . (Drawing 372). Drawing 372 shows the slave tube which allows each memory tube to be viewed remotely. Choice of position is obtained by use of a 40 position switch controlling the input from cathode followers from each memory position. These cathode followers are shown in Drawing 357.

4.3 READ- AROUND RATIO AND FLAWS.

Read-Around Ratio . It will be found to be desirable to

88

check the performance of the memory periodically. One of the performance tests is to use a routine which will go successively through the positions of the memory, bombarding each position with dashes after setting all surrounding addresses to dots, and noting dot to dash failures in these surrounding spots. The read-around ratio at any given spot is defined as the maximum number of times the spot may be bombarded without causing this type error. It will be found that there is a great tendency for most of the failures to occur at the edges and near large gaps in the raster. A typical run of such a test, observing all points, showed failures in the following total number of points out of the 40 x 1024 = 40,960 total.

READ-AROUND RATIO	TOTAL FAILURES
5	0
10	0
16	1
24	14
32	25
40	83

Flaws . The memory is also disturbed by the presence of flaws on the storage surface. In general these decrease the secondary electron ratio and cause a decrease in the dash output signals. When this situation becomes too critical, storage on these flaws becomes impractical and either the tube must be discarded, the raster must be moved off the flaw, or the coders must be told not to use the address in question. It has been found that there is a marked difference in the number of flaws on different tubes. At one time a plot

89

of the flaws on 40 tubes showed a total of 29 flaws of the trouble-
some size. However, the same check showed that there were 26 flaw-
less tubes.

To aid in avoiding flaws on the raster, two potentiometers
have been inserted in the deflection bus driver cathodes to allow
about one and half address motions both vertically and horizontally.
This enables the entire usuable raster to be scanned for flaw free
regions, and it is generally possible to avoid all flaws.

4.4 MEMORY ADJUSTMENT AND MAINTENANCE . To adjust the
memory the intensity should first be turned up until the dash signals
just begin to saturate the amplifier. (See Figure 4.5.)

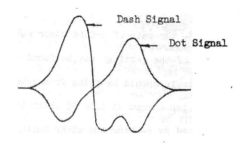

Figure 4.5

Dot and Dash Signals

Then the focus should be adjusted so that all the dash traces are as nearly coincident as possible in the sensing region as are all the dot signals. (See Figure 4.5). Then the astigmatism should be adjusted to improve on the focus adjustment if possible. A couple of repetitions of the focus-astigmatism adjustments should yield a reasonably sharp clean trace for the dash signals and dot signals which go very little above the base line in the positive dash region. After this the intensity should be adjusted up to a value which is as high as is compatible with no "fuzzing up" of the dot signals into the positive region of the dash where the sensing is done. It will be found that the response to changes in the intensity, focus and astigmatism settings will be rather sluggish due to the by-pass condensers on their leads. This is particularly true of the astigmatism adjustment. These adjustments should preferably be made with the machine carrying out a routine which puts a reversing pattern of dots and then dashes on the memory tubes. This can be done by setting the switch to "Order Pairs" and putting into R_3 the pair of orders clear subtract, store. A check on the accuracy of the settings may be found by observing the slave tube. All spots should be going from dots to dashes and back again in succession except on tube 39 which is all dots. Misadjustments may be noted by pushing the clear button, which forces the memory to all dots, and then observing whether any spot seems out of phase with its neighbors. The only ones which should be out of phase are those falling at the break in the pattern

91

where the clear was released.

Checking the Chassis in Place. Failures to write in dashes
may be caused by low intensity, flaws in the face of the tube or
possibly very poor focus or astigmatism adjustments. If the above
adjustments are correct, the amplifier may be faulty. A portion
of the logical circuitry may be at fault or the gain of the amplifier may seem to be insufficient.

To check the logical circuitry try to turn the tube to
all dashes by grounding lug 2 on the face of the tube, thus pulling
up on grid 7 of V6, Drawing 196. If dashes will not write in, the
logical circuitry, including the flipflop and its gates, is in all
probability at fault. If this operates correctly and the amplifier
output signals are of the proper shape, the amplifier gain is probably down. This is generally due to a loss of emission in the last
stage. Since this tube saturates when the output signal is positive,
loss of emission decreases the output signal to an unreliably low
value. Its effect is principally felt because the signal rises
too slowly for proper sensing. Changing the fourth amplifier stage
tube will generally correct the trouble.

In the event of a failure to write in a dash correctly from
the accumulator the input lead on lug number 4 on the front end of
the chassis may be grounded and another attempt made. A failure then
indicates a failure of the logical circuitry. By checking the chassis
output which is connected to the cathode of V16, the ability of the

chassis to produce the desired signal may be checked. By setting
all the inputs to the desired voltages, the output on pin C of
the back plug should be as shown in Figure 4.6.

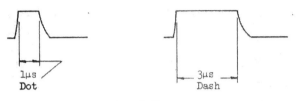

1μs
Dot

3μs
Dash

Figure 4.6
Pin C Outputs

When a cathode ray tube is picking up dashes randomly, there is
probably something physically wrong with the components of the chassis
unless the errors are common to other positions. These common errors
will be discussed later. The random errors will generally originate
in the chassis and it should be removed for repair.

If there are errors common to more than one cathode ray
tube, some single unit such as the address generator, pulsers, clock
or power supplies is probably at fault. It is easily seen that should
any of these vary too much, the memory would not work properly for
either so much noise would appear in the amplifier that errors would
result or the beam control logical circuitry would not be able to
operate as designed.

93

External Repairs . In repairing the removed chassis, a
number of more or less standard tests will usually locate the
trouble.   A voltage check of the amplifier condensers may be made
by putting about 300 volts in series with a voltmeter in series
with the 300 volt input while the chassis is disconnected, and then
checking to see that the voltmeter goes to 0. Very small leaks may
be found in this way, and these often are indicative of intermittent
spitting in one of the condensers or in some tube. Checking the
circuit diagram will show that this one check covers almost all of
the condensers in the chassis. The feed-through condensers also
are checked and are often a cause of trouble.

After this test the chassis may be finally checked in a
one-digit test memory. Here logical difficulties may be traced
through rather simply. Intermittent errors may be checked by tapping
the chassis and tubes and observing the occurrence of errors. These
will usually be dashes gained on a field of dots. It will be found
that the first amplifier stage will cause errors when tapped, even
in the case of good chassis. Other points should be free of mi-
crophonism with reasonable tapping.

CHAPTER 5

THE CONTROL

One of the principal components of any automatic computing machine is the control. The ORDVAC control consists of some 500 vacuum tubes located in 30 chassis. Most of these chassis are quite well localized, but a few, notably those associated with the end connections, are scattered through the arithmetic unit.

It is the function of the control to carry out the individual operations necessary for executing the orders which the programmer has combined into a routine for solving a problem. Because some of the orders require complicated sequencing and because there is a considerable variety of orders, the control is a highly interconnected component with very little duplication of circuits. This means that the connections between chassis are in many cases very numerous and that it is usually not possible to describe fully the operation of one of the control chassis without referring to elements of other chassis.

The control operates by withdrawing orders and numbers from the memory. In general it can be said that the control alternates the process of withdrawing pairs of orders with the process of executing them. Most of the work of the control is done between references to the memory. For example, all of the operations of arithmetic are handled by the control.

Thus in multiplication a number of steps must be carried out between the time the multiply order and the multiplicand come out
of the memory and the time the product is put back into the memory.
While it is impossible to separate completely the various control
functions, we shall in this manual discuss separately those operations which are and are not closely associated with action by the
memory.

Two kinds of drawings have been made for the control:
circuit drawings and logical drawings. It is usually very difficult
for a person unfamiliar with a schematic control circuit to under-
stand its operation, because it is laid out for simplicity in wiring.
For this reason reference to logical drawings will frequently be
made. The logical symbols used and their circuit equivalents are
given in Drawing 352. It will be found that nearly all circuit
elements are as shown, although exceptions occur occasionally.

The control chassis all have names, but in order to make
designations simpler each has been given a code letter. The names
and code letters are given in Table. 5.1.

Reference to tubes will be by code. Thus gate C63 is tube
63 in chassis C which is the Arithmetic Control Chassis. It is enabled by inverter C50 which gets its signal from cathode follower
J13.

5.1 THE ORDVAC ORDERS. It has already been said in Chapter
1 that the orders are stored in pairs in the memory, each memory
address being able to hold two 20-digit orders, a left hand (or

SYMBOL	COMPONENT	DRAWING NUMBER
A	Shift Sequencing Chassis	181,189,354
B	Arithmetic Stop Chassis	343,348
C	Arithmetic Control Chassis	244,300,380
D	Decoding Chassis	260,305
E	Driver III Chassis	171
F	Delay Selector Chassis	245,302
G	Carry Delay Chassis	236
H	Counter Output Chassis	253
J	End Connection Chassis	273,257
K	Complement Gate Driver Chassis	198
L	Input-Output Start and Shift Chassis II	271
M	Memory Control Chassis	289,301
N	Memory Synchronization Chassis	290,301
P	Register Selection Chassis	288,301
Q	Address Generator	195
S	Memory Pulser	368
T	Dispatch Counter	274
U	Input-Output Start and Shift Chassis I	326
V	Input-Output Relay Circuit	167
W	Video Amplifier	196
X	Input Transmitter-Distributor	174
Z	Interconnection Chassis-Input-Output	327
AA	Even Order Gate Chassis	251
BB	Odd Order Gate Chassis	250
CC	Odd Address Gate Chassis	249
DD	Even Address Cathode Follower Chassis	252

Table 5.1
Chassis Designations

even) order and a right hand (or odd) order.

Each order is in turn divided into two 10-digit parts, an instruction part and an address part. The address part is made up of the rightmost 10 digits of each order and the instruction part occupies the leftmost 9 digits. The 20th digit (2^{-9} or 2^{-29}) is unused.

The instruction part of an order is always sent to the Decoding Register for decoding. The decoding will be described in connection with the Decoding Chassis, and the manner of gating to this chassis will be described in connection with the Interplay Control.

The address part of an order can specify one of three things:

(1) A location in the memory from which a number will
   be taken or to which a number will be sent,

(2) A location in the memory from which an order will
   be taken,

(3) The number of shifts for a shift order.

In (1) the address goes to the Address Generator, in (2) it goes to the Control Counter, and in (3) it goes to the Recognition Circuits. The manner in which these transfers are handled is described under the components mentioned. For the present it is necessary only to know that these three possibilities exist and that only the left hand (even) address is connected to the 3 places mentioned. The odd address is gated to the even location by the odd Address Gate when it is needed.

98

A convenient separation of the orders into groups may be made as follows:

    I. Arithmetic Orders

        (a) The 8 addition orders

        (b) The 3 multiplication orders

        (c) Division

    II. The 8 A Orders

    III. The Shift Orders

        (a) Left Shift,

        (b) Right Shift,

    IV. The Input-Output Orders

        (a) Read in from the tape, T

        (b) Read out to the printer, P

    V. Store Orders

        (a) Write into the memory, M

        (b) Write partially into the memory, E, E'

    VI. Control Transfer Orders

        (a) Unconditional transfer, U, U'

        (b) Conditional transfer, C, C'

        (c) Stop, Z

    VII. The R Order

The foregoing grouping of the orders was made because of common properties they possess. These properties are as follows:

    I. The Arithmetic Orders all require a readout of a number from the memory into R^3 as part of the order. They all require shifts in the registers in their execution. The addresses all go to the address generator.

II. The A Orders are identical with the addition orders as far as execution in the arithmetic unit is concerned and are different in that instead of coming from the memory the addend (or subtrahend) comes from R_2. A memory readout cycle is used for the transfer from R_2 to R^3. The addresses go to the control counter.

III. The Shift Orders in their execution are often the same as certain steps in the Arithmetic and A orders. Their addresses are sent to the recognition circuit.

IV. The Input-Output Orders are primarily shift orders and are treated in much the same way. The addresses go to the recognition circuit.

V. The Store Orders are the only ones which write into the memory. They involve no shifting. Their addresses go to the address generator.

VI. The Control Transfer Orders are logical in nature. They cause neither memory action nor shifting. Their addresses go to the control counter.

VII. The R Order requires a memory readout into R_2 and is actually, except for the register to which it communicates, the same as the first part of any Arithmetic Order. Its address goes to the address generator.

5.2 PRINCIPLES OF OPERATION OF THE CONTROL. The ORDVAC control is asynchronous. There is no over-all timing device, and each operation of the control is carried out only when it receives a signal that the preceding one has been finished. Most of the sequences therefore require a closed loop in order to carry out repetitive operations. The fundamental principle which has been adhered to in the design of the control is that its operation must be reliable. Consequently a number of "safety features" have been included, being paid for in speed.

The use of one flipflop F to sequence a pair of operations illustrates the functioning of an asynchronous system. Let the two operations be designated A and B, as shown in Figure 5.1.

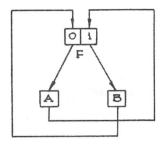

Figure 5.1 Simple Sequencing

When F = 0, A occurs, causing F to turn to 1 and initiate B. This returns F to 0, and the steps are repeated. This simple example clearly has defects. For one thing, when F goes to 1 it turns off A and starts B. It is possible that A may not be completely off when B begins, and trouble can occur if the two are related, as when A is clearing a register and B is gating to the same register. This can be avoided by putting on safety circuits

101

as shown in Figure 5.2

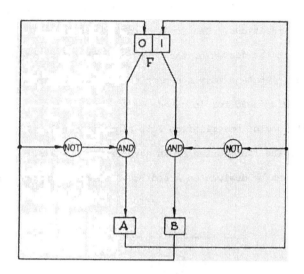

Figure 5.2

Safety Circuits for Sequencing

When A occurs F is turned to 1 as before, and this shuts
off A. But now B cannot go, because of the "not" circuit, until
A is off. The same thing holds for the other state. This is a common
device for assuring that an operation is off, and it is frequently
used when it is necessary to know that a signal such as a gate signal has gone down and is back up again.

Another principle is that of sensing the last moving element
of an operation whenever possible. This is illustrated in Fig. 5.3
for the case of a flipflop and gate, where it is of particular im-

portance.

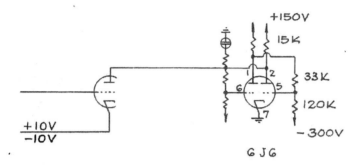

Figure 5.3

Flipflop and Gate

Let us suppose that pin 2 is high so that the flipflop is in the 1
state. We want to turn it to 0 and to sense when it has turned.
When the gate conducts, the voltage on pin 2 starts to fall, as does
that on pin 6. This causes the voltage on pin 1 to rise and brings
up the voltage on pin 5. The obvious place to sense is pin 6 since
it is negative for 0 and we use negative signals.[¥] But this would
be dangerous because the flipflop may not be completely turned when

---

[¥] With few exceptions the ORDVAC control uses negative voltages
to initiate operations.

pin 6 enables the sensing tube, and something may occur to prevent its turning.

We therefore sense from pin 5 with an inverter, as shown in Figure 5.4. Because of the cutoff characteristics of the tubes, the inverter cannot supply an output signal until the voltage at pin 5 has risen to a value which assures that the flipflop has turned over.

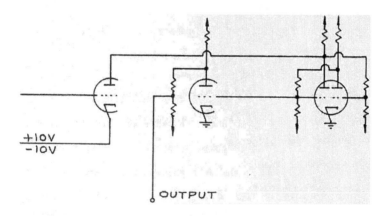

Figure 5.4

Flipflop Sensing for Safe Operation

104

PART I

PRINCIPAL CONTROL ELEMENTS FOR ARITHMETIC

We shall be primarily concerned here with orders listed in categories I, II, III, and IV of Section 5.1. They are carried out by using registers, the adder and digit resolver, and a number of control chassis. The control chassis involved carry out the operations by sequencing appropriately the clearing and gating operations in the registers and the gate from the adder.

We shall assume here that the proper operands have been put into the registers and that we need consider the address part of an order only for those orders in III and IV.

The discussion of how the operands get into the registers and how the addresses of orders are handled will be given in Part II, the Interplay Control.

5.3 SHIFT SEQUENCING CHASSIS.(Drawings 181, 189, 354). It is the function of this chassis to perform the sequencing operations which control shifts in R_1 and R_2 . It goes through the four steps which are necessary to shift R_1 (and the slave R_2) right or left or to admit information from the digit resolver into R^1 and shift it right or left into R_1 (R_2 following as before).

The sequences which this chassis carries out are given in Table 5.2.

OPERATION	R_I SEQUENCE	R_{II} SEQUENCE
(1) Shift right	BCR^1, YGR^1 YCR_1, BGR_1	BCR^2, YGR^2 YCR_2, BGR_2
(2) Shift left	BCR^1, YGR^1 GCR_1, RGR_1	BCR^2, YGR^2 GCR_2, RGR_2
(3) Enter from digit resolver and shift right	RCR^1, GGR^1 YCR_1, BGR_1	Same as (1)
(4) Enter from digit resolver and shift left	RCR^1, GGR^1 GCR_1, RGR_1	Same as (2)

Table 5.2

Sequences in Shift Sequencing Chassis

There are four steps necessary for a shift - two clears and two gates. These steps are carried out by a pair of flip-flops which proceed successively through the states 11, 10, 00 and 01, repeating as many times as is required. As each step is completed one of the flipflops is changed to initiate the next step.

The sequencing of the four operations making up the shifts described in Table 5.2 is fundamental to all arithmetic operations. Much of the remainder of the control is devoted to supplying information to the shift sequencing chassis.

Two flipflops A18 and A21 (referred to sometimes as Tc and Tg, the subscripts standing for "clear" and "gate") carry out the sequencing in a manner analogous to that described in Section 5.2. Since as shown in Table 5.2, there are actually four sequences, each having four steps in R_I, more information than that given by T_c and T_g is needed, and this information is furnished from the decoding chassis by the signals L and R of D58 and from the arithmetic control chassis by the signals "0" and "1" coming from C44 and C8, respectively.

The output signals from the shift sequencing chassis operate the registers, but not directly. They go through intermediate chassis (the clear driver drivers, the clear and gate drivers and the Driver III chassis)which supply the necessary power and voltage levels for clearing and gating and which, in the case of the Driver III chassis, do some limited logic.

Moreover, even the signals to these chassis are not always direct. For if the adder is being used we must make the machine wait for carries before gating the result of the addition into R^1. Therefore there are outputs to the Delay Selector and inputs from the Carry Delay.

The clears and gates in the shift sequencing chassis always work in pairs. Thus we always have RC-GG, BC-YG, GC-RG, and YC-BG.

The rest positions for toggles T_c and T_g are the states 1,1. These are the states for RC or BC. The other states are given in Table 5.3. Rather than describe the behavior of every possible sequence in this chassis, we shall choose the case in which we have the signals R and "1". We shall then create the sequence RCR^1, GGR^1, YCR_1, BGR_1 and the slave sequence BCR^2, YGR^2, YCR_2, BGR_2. It will then be quite clear how the chassis works. (Refer to Drawing 354).

If we have the states $T_c = 1$, $T_g = 1$, and "1", and if the signal E4 (RGR_2 or BGR_2) is off, then the signal RCR^1 goes from A6 to register R^1 by the way of clear driver driver and clear driver chassis. It sets flipflop F3 to 1. When the R^1 clear bus goes down, two signals go from it to the Delay Selector, one via the "on" circuit E1. As described in Section 5.7, a delay will occur and the control waits for it. When it comes, there is an output to BCR^2. This will turn T_c to 0 at pin 7 of A12, shutting off RCR^1 and thus, through a chain of chassis, shutting off BCR^2. When BCR^2 comes back up GGR^1 is enabled because flipflop F3 supplies a GG enable signal and disables YGR^1. From A13 a signal goes through the R_1 gate driver and causes GGR^1. This causes YGR^2 via OR circuit E3 which (in addition to sending a "down" signal to the shift counter and resetting toggle F1) turns T_g to 0 by way of gate A20.

T_c	T_g	OPERATION
1	1	RC or BC
0	1	GG or YG
0	0	YC or GC
1	0	BG or RG

Table 5.3

Tc and Tg States

This turns off GGR^1 and YGR^2 and results in YCR_1 when YGR^1 goes off. The slave YCR_2 will turn T_c back to "1", thus shutting off the clear and enabling BGR_1. This will proceed precisely as YGR^1 did, and BGR_2 will send an "up" signal to the shift counter and a signal to gate A23 by way of "or" circuit E4 and cathode follower E5. The gate will turn T_g to 1, and when BGR_2 goes off the circuit is in its original state and ready to start another sequence.

Safety Features of the Shift Sequencing Chassis. It is important that some kind of assurance be had that the operations ordered have been carried out. This is done in one of several ways:

109

1. The method of turning over T_c and T_g is the same as that used in the registers.

2. The turnover requirements of T_c and T_g are more stringent than those of register flipflops, so that if the register flipflops do not operate neither will the corresponding control flipflop.

3. The signal for an operation shall require that the preceding operation has occurred and has been turned off.

4. The signal from a control flipflop shall be used only when the flipflop has been positively turned over.

Let us consider T_c, which is turned by a clearing technique like that used in the registers. (Refer to Drawing 189). Suppose that it is in the 1 state and that BCR^1 has been enabled. This will result in a voltage drop at pin 7 of A12 when BCR^2 goes down and, because of the bleeder at pin 7, it will not let the plate supply to pin 1 of T_c drop as far as the register plates did. So T_c will not turn over if the register flipflops did not. The lowering of the voltage at pin 1 of T_c turns T_c to 0.

The turning of T_c causes pin 6 to rise from -37v to 0v, resulting in a negative output from the inverter A11a. It is important to note that pin 6 is the last moving point of T_c and that the output of inverter A11b will not move (because of the tube cutoff characteristic) until pin 6 of A18 has risen to approximately -4v. This makes it certain that no signal comes from A11b until T_c is positively turned over and A18, in turn, will not turn if the register voltages are insufficient to turn the register flipflops. This assurance would not be had if the signal were taken from pin 5 of A18.

The output of A11a causes pin 6 of A7 and pin 5 of A8 to go negative. When pin 6 of A7 goes negative, the output of the inverter 7a rises and the black clear signal is shut off at pin 5 of A4. This causes pin 6 of A12 to rise again, indicating that the clear has been shut off. As a result pin 5 of A7 will rise, causing the output of inverter 7b to fall and making pin 6 of A8 negative. Since A8 is an "and" circuit, pin 7 now goes negative and supplies a signal for the next step, in this case the Yellow Gate.

Let us consider T_g which is A21. Suppose that it is in the O state and that a black gate is on. This means that pin 2 of gate tube A23 is pulled down. Since the grid is pegged at -5V, this gate will not operate until the cathode is at about -7V. However, the register gates will operate at about -2V, so that we are assured that T_g will not turn over if the register gate voltage is insufficient to turn the register flipflops.

The turning of T_g to 1 results in a negative signal from the inverter 22b caused by the rise of the last moving point (pin 6) of T_g. This, through cathode follower A23b and inverter A25b, shuts off the black gate at pin 5 of A27. Pin 6 of A24 then goes positive. Since pin 5 of A24 is pegged at +5V, the voltage of pin 6 must be at least +1V before the left side of the

111

tube begins to conduct, assuring us that the gate is off. The output of A24, upon going negative, enables the following clear, either RCR^1 or BCR^1 as the case may be.

Test Switches In The Shift Sequencing Chassis. The control can be interrupted in any operation which is using the shift sequencing chassis merely by preventing the turnover of one of the flipflops T_c or T_g. For this purpose four toggle switches are mounted at the left hand end of the registers. They are connected to pins 2 and 7 of A12 and to pin 8 of A20 and pin 2 of A23 as shown in Drawing 189. By opening any one of these switches the clear or gate in whose turnoff line the switch is located will be left on and the operation will stop. The operation will continue if the switch is closed. These switches provide a very valuable test tool for the maintenance man.

The remaining parts of the control associated with the orders under discussion are concerned primarily with supplying the proper information to the shift sequencing chassis so that appropriate clearing and gating can be performed.

5.4 SHIFT COUNTER, (Drawing 113). The shift counter is a 6-stage counter with the function of keeping track of the number of steps in multiplication, division, in the shift orders, and the input-output orders.

It consists of two banks of flipflops and gates. The lower bank of flipflops is the counting row of the counter. Two pulses are required for each count, a down pulse from YGR^2 cathode and an up pulse from RGR_2 or BGR_2 (See Drawings 189, 171, and 354).

Unless the up and down pulses alternate, no counting will be done. A logical diagram is shown in Figure 5.5.

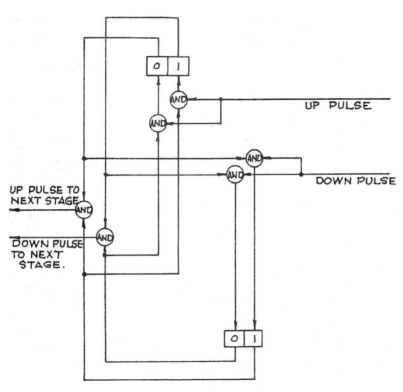

Figure 5.5

Logical Diagram of Shift Counter

In operation the counter has both rows of flipflops cleared to 0 by the counter reset bus (Drawing 232), which is the plate supply to pin 2 of each counter flipflop. The counting begins with a "down" input which gates 1 into the lower row of Col. 1, (the 2^0 stage) since the down gates are crossed. This 0-1

113

combination in the first stage will cause an up gate in the 2^1 stage, but this does nothing since it gates 0 to 0. The first "up" input then gates 1 into the top row of Col.1. The second "down" input gates 0 into the lower row of Col. 1, and this 1-0 combination causes a "down" date in Col. 2 which puts 1 into the lower row of Col. 2. The counter has now counted to 000010, which is 2 in decimal representation. The counting proceeds in this way.

5.5 RECOGNITION CIRCUIT (Drawings 260,305). The recognition circuit is used to signal the end of an operation using the shift counter when the shift counter reaches a pre-assigned value. This circuit occupies 14 tubes in the decoding chassis, D21, D22, and D1 to D12.

The recognition circuit is connected to the right-hand 6 address digits of the left hand order, these being the digits used to indicate the number of shifts desired. When the number in these digits agrees with that in the shift counter, a counter recognition signal is given if the order is in Group III or IV.

The recognition signal will also be given on multiply and divide orders when the counter reaches 39.

Operation of the circuit is shown in Drawing 305. The counter is set to 0, and a recognition signal will be given whenever all inputs to the 6 input "or" circuit are positive. For orders involving shifts the output of D43 is negative and there is recognition when the counter and the last six digits

114

of the left hand address location agree.

It should be-noted that for a given setting of the even address flipflops there is more than one Shift Counter value which will cause recognition. However, the correct value is always the first one reached by the Shift Counter, so there can never be an incorrect comparison.

If a shift is not involved, the output of D43 is positive and the number 39 is supplied for comparison with the counter.

The recognition signal goes to B7 of the arithmetic stop chassis (Drawing 343).

5.6 ARITHMETIC STOP CHASSIS.(Drawings 343, 348). This chassis performs several functions. It contains the circuits for stopping arithmetic operations, for supplying the shift counter reset signals, and for actually resetting the shift counter. It furnishes an end of operation signal to the control for the orders which involve the shift sequencing chassis. It also contains the circuits which handle the sequencing necessary to follow multiplication immediately by subtraction when a negative multiplier correction is required.

The chassis contains four flipflops, and at a time when the chassis is not being used these flipflops are in the states shown in Col. 3 of Table 5.4.

When an operation using the arithmetic stop chassis is ordered, a reset enable signal comes from M35 to B9, and with B4 and B14 set properly gate B19 opens and causes the counter

115

reset bus to go down.

FLIPFLOP	LOCATION	QUIESCENT STATE	BEGINNING OF ARITH. OPERATION
Stop	B1	0	1
False Control	B4	0	0
End	B6	1	1
Reset	B14	1	0

Table 5.4

Flipflops in Arithmetic Stop Chassis

This turns stop flipflop B1 to 1 and, via inverter B19, turns reset flipflop B14 to 0, shutting off the reset and letting the computer reset bus come back up. By now the three grids of B15 and B24a are negative, and the operation will begin as soon as one more input to this "and" circuit goes negative. This input is "go enable" from M71b and comes into the arithmetic stop chassis to the cathodes of B15 and B24a. It also goes to the grids of C10. It may go negative at the same time as the reset enable when there is no wait for memory action, or it may have to wait for the memory.

On the go enable the grids of C10 go negative and the appropriate "0" or "1" wire to the shift sequencing chassis is pulled down, starting the arithmetic operation (or shift operation). The flipflops of the arithmetic stop chassis are then in the

116

states shown in Col. 4 of Table 5.3.

If the operation is an addition order or A order, the stop signal comes on $\overline{YGR}^1$. If it is one of the multiply, divide, shift or input-output orders, the stop signal comes from the recognition circuit, but this comes within about 2 microseconds of YGR^2 since YGR^2 supplies the shift counter down signal. The essential point is that the stop signal comes early enough to turn over B1 and assure the stop.

The turnover of B1 is by the OR circuit gate B7. When B1 turns to 0, the go enable at B15 goes positive, pulling up the grids of C10 and inhibiting the "0" and "1" signals. The operation cannot proceed after RGR_2 or BGR_2, which is what is wanted.

One input to the circuit B18a is made positive by the turnover of B1. The other, via inverter B5, goes positive when RGR_2 or BGR_2 goes down. This then turns end flipflop B6 to 0 via gate B12a since B18 is acting as a positive "and" circuit. When RGR_2 or BGR_2 goes off again, B5 goes back negative and a "B" end enable is supplied by B3 to M9.

If there is no multiplication correction, there will now be a control sequence and the input to pin 5 of B2 will rise. This will operate gates B17 and turn B6 and B14 to 1. The turnover of these flipflops operates the positive "and" circuit B24 and tries to turn the False Control flipflop B4 to 0 (it is already 0) through the circuit B11, B10a, B5. The "B" end enable is

117

turned off by B6, releasing the gate signal to B10a. There is
also supplied a signal "B op turnover enable" from B10b which
furnishes a check on the turnover of B6 and B14. If they do not
both turn, this signal, which goes to C64b, will inhibit the return to an operation sequence and hang up the machine. It should
also be noted that unless the flipflop B4 is returned to 0
(assuming it had been 1) the go enable will be inhibited on the
next order involving this chassis and the machine will hang up.

If there is a multiplication correction, the "B end enable"
B3 goes negative as usual after the first part of the multiplication,
but no end signal gets past M9, and M8 sends back a "false control
turnover" turning B4 to 1 by gate B10.

This now has the same effect on B6 and B14 as turnover to
"control" since it turns them both to 1 by pulling up B2 and operating gates B17. The turning of these toggles therefore turns B4.
The reset enable and go enable signals from M35 and M71b are still
on, so the subtraction proceeds normally and there is now no
difference between this and any other subtraction. At the end the
multiplication correction flipflop C62 will have been returned to 1,
allowing the end enable signal from B3 to pass through "and" circuit
M9.

5.7 <u>CARRY DELAY</u> (Drawing 236) <u>AND DELAY SELECTOR</u> (Drawings 245, 302). Because the adder is continually connected to R^3
and R_1, a certain minimum time must be permitted after changing

the contents of either of these registers before information may be taken from the adder. This is the longer of the carry propagate and carry collapse times. In ORDVAC the carry collapse time is 9 1/2 microseconds and the carry time allowed is 13 microseconds.

This delay is created in the carry delay chassis, and the determination of when it occurs is made in the delay selector chassis. The two chassis will be considered together.

If it were not for division, the handling of the delay would be much simpler than it is. On all other operations the delay can be initiated with RCR^1 since the gate from the adder, GGR^1, always follows RCR^1. But in division it is necessary to perform the addition before it is known whether or not the result will be used. Therefore every division operation, whether it begins with RCR^1 or BCR^1, must start the delay.

There are thus two inputs to the delay selector: BCR^1 and divide in F7 and RCR^1 in F8. Either of these, by gate F9 turns flip-flop F1 to 1, this flipflop having previously been returned to 0 by the YGR^2 which occurs in any arithmetic operation. The turning of F1 sends a negative signal to G5, pulling the cathode of G7 positive and cutting off the current through diode G2b. This will cause the 50μμf condenser on the delay multivibrator G4 to discharge, and pin 5 of G4 will go negative after a delay, producing a positive output signal from G8. This signal is then supplied to inverter F11, causing F12 to be enabled since either RCR^1 or BCR^1 is still on.

The output of F12 goes to F10 which then enables BCR^2 and permits the operation to continue.

If there is no divide order, then BCR^1 implies no delay and we do not wait. This is handled by a signal from inverter F4 when there is no divide order. Then F6 is enabled on BCR^1, opening gate F5 and enabling F12. This then sends a signal to enable BCR^2 as before.

The flipflop F3 is a safety device to make it impossible for the wrong gate to follow a clear in R^1. It is set to 1 by RCR^1 and to 0 by BCR^1. When it is set to 1, an enable signal goes to A14 for GGR^1 and a disable signal goes to A16 for YGR^1. The reverse happens when it is set to 0.

5.8 <u>DECODING CHASSIS</u>. (Drawings 260, 305, 306). The decoding chassis is a 72 tube chassis which has the function of decoding the orders and which also contains the counter recognition circuit. The decoding chassis contains a decoding register of 10 flipflops, referred to as R_4, nine of which are used. By means of the even and odd order gates (Drawings 250, 251) the left or right hand orders can be gated to R_4 from R_3. This gating is described in connection with the interplay control.

There is no complete matrix for decoding orders. Rather, there are several small matrices combined in various ways. This results in a large number of combinations which can produce useful orders in the machine.

120

The locations of the R_4 flipflops and their principal functions are shown in Drawing 306.

With one exception the gating to these flipflops is directly from R_3 via the even and odd order gates. This exception is the gate to D70. For reasons of logical safety there is a flipflop C37 in the arithmetic control which is closely associated with D70. Since C37 must be in the proper state, the gate to D70 is operated by gating to C37 from R_3 and then turning D70 over with C37.

The dots on Drawing 306 shows which flipflops are sensed for any particular order. Table 5.5 gives a brief indication of the function of each flipflop in R_4.

It will be noted that the flipflops in R_4 are not arranged in the same order as in R_3. (Drawing 307) This is because the simplest wiring arrangement in R_4 is not the best arrangement for coding.

The logical structure of the decoding chassis is shown in Drawing 305. In addition to the 9 flipflops previously described, use is made of 2 flipflops outside the chassis. One of these, 2^0R_1, is the sign digit in R_1, which has to be sensed for the conditional transfer orders C and C'. The second is the control-operate flipflop, N15 in the memory synchronization chassis (Drawing 290 and 301). Instructions are transferred to R_4 during a "control sequence and no order is executed until the "operate sequence (See Section 5.11),

NAME	TUBE	FUNCTION
Roundoff	D62	It determines whether or not 2^{-1} will be inserted in R_1 prior to the carrying out of any order. The insertion of 2^{-1} requires that D65 be set to "clear". Otherwise the arithmetic unit will not proceed.
+ - Number - A.V.	D63 D64	These flipflops with the sign of R^3, set the complement gate and are also used in a matrix for certain orders in which the complement gate setting is immaterial. These orders are U, C', M, E and E'.
Clear - Hold	D65	This flipflop if set to "1" signals a clear in R_1 before any operation continues, and it must be returned to "0" before continuing.
R_2 - Not	D66	This is used in a number of matrices and determines primarily whether the order is one dealing with R_2 or not. It is sensed on all orders except M, E and E'.

These flipflops are sensed on every order, their 4 states having the following meanings:

Use Mem-Not	D67	1 1	Use Memory, read out
Read-Order; Write- Shift	D68	1 0	Use memory, write in
		0 1	Do not use memory, send address to order counter.
		0 0	Do not use memory, send address to shift counter.

+ X	D69	This is primarily intended to distinguish between the add orders and the multiply, divide orders. It is also sensed in P, T, and U'.
R - L	D70	This is the flipflop which distinguishes between left and right shifts and which supplies the L, R signals to the Shift Sequencing Chassis.

Table 5.5

Decoding Register Flipflops

thus assuring that all flipflops in R_4 have been set before going ahead. A few orders are connected to the control-operate flip-flop in the memory control chassis (Drawing 289) instead of in the decoding chassis.

The logic of the decoding chassis is straightforward and requires only one comment. This is with regard to the M, E and E' orders. Because of the way these are handled in the memory control chassis, a positive rather than negative logic has been used. On the M order, for example, flipflop D64 is set to 0. This gives a positive signal out for M.

5.9 ARITHMETIC CONTROL (Drawing 244). The carrying out of an arithmetic operation consists entirely of manipulating numbers through proper use of the shift sequencing chassis, the complement gate and the carry delay. By appropriate shifting, admission to the adder, and removal from the adder any arithmetic can be performed. It is the function of the arithmetic control to supply instructions to the shift sequencing chassis, for it is in the arithmetic control that the logic for the addition orders, multiplication, division, multiplication corrections, and roundoff is carried out.

CLEARING R_1 AND MULTIPLICATION ROUNDOFF. Many orders require that R_1 be cleared to 0 at the start of the order. The multiplication roundoff consists of clearing R_1 to 0 and gating 1 to $2^{-1} R_1$ before doing the multiplication. Consequently, the operations "clear" and "roundoff" are closely related.

The clear is a YCR_1 and is ordered by the clear-hold flipflop

123

D65. The roundoff is ordered by D62. Before any arithmetic operation can proceed both D65 and D62 must have been returned to the 0
state. If the order to round off without clearing is given, ORDVAC
will hang up.

Let us suppose we have the clear and roundoff ordered. Then
flipflops D62, D65 and C66 are all in the "1" state, the latter having
been set to 1 by the gating from R_3 to R_4 which always precedes an
arithmetic operation. When N15 turns to operate, the "and" C5
goes negative, opens gate A16 and creates YCR_1 by way of A36. A
slave YCR_2 is prevented by H4 and H6, for if D65 is a 1, pin 3 of
H6 is held up. Nothing further happens in the Shift Sequencing
Chassis because A18 (T_c) must be turned by YCR_2.

On YCR_1 D66 is turned to 0, shutting off YCR_1. When YCR_1
is back up, inverter C16a supplies the enabling signal to C54 which
returns D65 to 0. If there had been no roundoff the operation would
have proceeded, D49 and D61 having been enabled.

With a roundoff C54 causes a 1 to be gated into $2^{-1}R_1$. This
is done by the lower gate in the 2^{-3} column of R_{III} (See insert,
Drawing 359). This tube is otherwise unused. Since pin 6 of this
gate is positive because of the state of D62, the gate operates. When
$2^{-1}R_1$ is fully turned to 1, the inverter in Col. 7 of R_I operates and
via the "and" of Col. 9 operates gate D59 which returns D62 to 0. The
operation then proceeds.

Notice what happens if D62 is not returned to 0. Then the
grids of C44 are held up so that no 0 or 1 signal can go to the Shift

Sequencing chassis. The machine stops if an order using the chassis is involved. Notice also that a roundoff without a clear will cause ORDVAC to hang up because there is no return of D62 to 0.

Addition and Subtraction. There are 8 addition orders distinguished by choices from 3 sets of alternatives: (1) Clear or do not clear R_1, (2) add or subtract, and (3) use the number or its absolute value. The latter two categories determine the four orders which are add, subtract, add absolute value, and subtract absolute value. Their execution requires setting the complement gate properly and then carrying out the 8 operations RC, GG, YC, BG, BC, YG, GC, RG in R_1 and the corresponding slave operations in R_{II}. The last 4 steps are, of course, a left shift required because the shift from R^1 to R_1 was down right instead of straight down.

The complement gate is set by the outputs of C1, 2, 3 and 4 through the "or" circuit C30. The output C30 is negative if a subtraction is required; otherwise it is positive. It is negative if we:

1. Subtract any number,

2. Add the absolute value of a negative number,

3. Subtract the absolute value of a positive number.

The complement gate (drawing 155) has two inputs of opposite polarity, each of which is supplied by one of a pair of complement gate drivers (Drawing 198).

The end around carry (Section 2.9) must also be provided for in order to supply a true complement. This is done by putting a carry signal

125

from the complement gate bus into the otherwise unused carry input of the first stage of the adder. Two unused tubes in column 1 of the adder (Drawing 104) are used for this. When the complement gate is set for subtract, the right hand side of the tube in Row 3, Column 1 conducts and the current through the 18k resistor on the first stage of the adder produces a carry input.

If the output of C30 is positive, the inverter C40b supplies the required negative signal and the complement gate is set to "add". As a check, the gate C27 turns flipflop C28 to 1, and via inverter C29a this is compared in the "and" circuit C31 with the signal supplied to the complement gate driver. A similar check is made in C33 for the opposite setting. If the check is all right, C32 goes negative and C22 is enabled.

Part of the instruction for the ADD orders is to set D70 to 1, i.e., the L-R signal to R. Therefore C21 and C8 are enabled and the signal "1" goes to A2. (See Drawing 189). This initiates the sequence RC, GG, YC, BG, in R_I.

A special provision must be made for the last digits, 2^{-39}, in R^1 and R_2, for they will be lost on a right shift if they are not stored somewhere. Without exception, $2^{-39}R^1$ goes to $2^{-1}R_2$ on BGR_1, this digit having been vacated by the slave shift in R_2 which does not shift the sign digit. The gate which performs this is J10b (Drawings 273, 357) which is enabled by BGR_1 and gets its grid signal from $2^{-39}R^1$ via cathode follower J6b.

The content of $2^{-39}R_2$ is stored in J16. On BGR_2 $2^{-39}R_2$ is

126

always transferred to J16 by the BG in the last stage of R_{II}, a normally unused gate. This storage is needed so that R_2 will be unaltered during the addition orders.

On BGR_1 if there is a "not recognize" signal on C46, C15 is enabled, turning flipflop C37 to 0, C37 having been left in the 1 state by any previous addition.

The "not recognize" signal is needed to prevent the turnover of V37 on BGR_1 at the end of the positive part of a multiplication with a multiplier correction. (See below). For in this case the Decoding Register has been changed to "subtract" before the multiplication ends. This enables C39 when A21 (T_g) has turned to 1, which is on the BGR^2 or RGR_2. The output of C39, by gate C17b, turns D70 (L-R) to 0, giving the signal L. This results in enabling C19 which supplies a "0" signal to A4 and initiates the left shift sequence. It may look here as if another RCR^1 could occur if the "0" signal did not come along quickly enough. This is true. But the BCR^1 will follow immediately when the "0" signal does come, and the flip-flop F3 (See delay selector) assures that the proper gate will follow. On RGR_1 C13 opens gate C14a and turns C37 back to "1". Meanwhile on YGR^1 gate B7 has opened to stop the addition, and the stop will occur after RGR_2. An end of operation signal is supplied from B3 to N9.

During the left shift of addition, we must replace the information which has been temporarily stored in $2^{-1}R_2$ and in J16.

This is done on RGR_2.

The gating from $2^{-1}R^2$ and J16 on RGR_2 is not the same for all orders.

Let us first consider J16. It is gated back into $2^{-39}R_2$ only on the addition and A orders (which the control sees as addition orders when the gating to R^3 is completed). Otherwise $2^{-39}R_2$ on addition is made by gate J17a which is enabled by the "and" circuit J18.

Now let us consider the gating from $2^{-1}R^2$ on RGR_2. On every order involving RGR_2 except the addition or A orders, a left shift transfers the contents of $2^{-1}R_2$ into 2^0R_2. But on these orders the left shift transfers the contents of $2^{-1}R_2$ into $2^{-39}R_1$. This is done by J9 and J10. When $2^{-1}R_2 = 0$, pin 5 is at ground and the cathode of J9 is positive. This gates 0 into $2^{-39}R_1$ on RGR_2. Similarly, if there is no addition or A order, pin 5 of J9 is positive and RGR_2 puts 0 into $2^{-39}R_1$. But if $2^{-1}R^2 = 1$ and there is an addition or A order, pin 7 of J9 is negative and RGR_2 does not change $2^{-39}R_1$ from the 1 it was set to on the preceding GCR_1.

The A Orders. These orders, given in Group II of Section 5.1 are the ones which transfer from R_2 to R_1. They operate by transferring first to R^3 and then following the identical procedure of one of the 8 addition orders. The manner in which the transfer to R^3 is made from R_2 is precisely the same as that in which it is made to R^3 from the memory, and memory pulses are used for the operation. (See Interplay Control).

Referring to Drawing 305 of the decoding chassis logic, it is seen that the add order, coming from D23, is actually an OR on the true addition orders, D45, and the A orders, D25a. Either of these on receipt of the proper initiating signal which somes after a transfer to R^3, will cause the same sequence to be executed.

Multiplication. For a description of the logic of multiplication, see Chapter 1. In ORDVAC the multiplication is carried out (a) by adding the multiplicand, held in R^3, to previously accumulated partial products in R_2 and dividing by 2, or (b) by merely dividing the previously accumulated partial products by 2, depending upon whether or not the multiplier digit being inspected is 1 or 0. After 39 steps the operation stops if the multiplier sign digit $2^0 R_2$ is 0. If $2^0 R_2$ is 1, the multiplicand must be subtracted from the accumulated partial products.

The process requires that 4 digits be inspected at each step of the operation. These digits are $2^{-39} R_2$, $2^0 R^3$, $2^0 R_1$ and $2^0 R^1$.

The procedure is as follows:

(1) On each of the 39 steps required inspect $2^{-39} R_2$.

    (a) If $2^{-39} R_2 = 0$, shift R_1 and R_2 one place to the right by executing the sequence BC, YG, YC, BG in R_I and R_{II}. Inspect $2^0 R_1$, $2^0 R^1$, and $2^0 R^3$. If 2 or 3 of them are 1, gate 1 into $2^0 R_1$ on BGR_1. Otherwise do nothing, which will leave $2^0 R_1 = 0$.

    (b) If $2^{-39} R_2 = 1$, add R^3, with sign, to R_1 and shift the sum one place to the right, shifting R_2 one place to the right at the same time by executing the sequences RC, GG, YC, BG in R_I and

129

BC, YG, YC, BG in R_{II}. Then proceed as in (a).

(2) After the 39th step subtract R^3 from R_1 if $2^0R_2 = 1$.

(3) After (2) make $2^0R_2 = 0$ so that the least significant 39 digits of the product will not have a negative sign attached to them.

It is evident that the inspection of 2^0R_1 just before BGR_1 requires that it be stored some place, because YCR_1 will destroy it. Therefore on YGR^1 or GGR^1 2^0R_1 is gated into 2^0R^2, a flipflop which is otherwise unused. We therefore inspect 2^0R^3, 2^0R^1 and 2^0R^2 prior to BGR_1.

The digit $2^{-39}R_2$ is sensed by J15 and the outputs go to C7 for 0 and C9 for 1. By means of the "or" circuits C8 or C20 the proper "0" or "1" signal is supplied to the Shift Sequencing Chassis.

At each YGR^2 and BGR^2 signals are supplied to the shift counter.

On YGR^1 or GGR^1 2^0R^2, 2^0R^3 and 2^0R^1 are then inspected in 12, 23 and 24. If any two or three are negative C35 is enabled on the BGR_1 and gate tube C34 makes 2^0R_1 (cleared by YCR_1) a 1. At each right shift in multiplication the digit in $2^{-39}R_2$ is lost. At the same time the content of $2^{-39}R_1$ is shifted into $2^{-1}R_2$. This results in having the 78 digits of the product arranged with a sign and 39 digits in R_1 and the remaining 39 digits in R_2, the sign digit in R_2 being ignored.

When the shift counter reaches 39, the recognition circuit (Section 5.4) supplies a signal to stop the multiplication. If

$2^0 R_2 = 0$, the operation is over.

But if $2^0 R_2 = 1$, a negative multiplier correction, a (subtraction is required. This correction necessitates a major alteration in the normal sequencing of the computer. For each execution of an order is ordinarily followed by a control sequence devoted to handling another order. In multiplication correction we have what amounts to two orders (multiplication and subtraction) in succession without an intervening control operation.

In the arithmetic stop chassis is a flipflop B4, called the "false control" flipflop which plays the role of the "operation-control" flipflop N15 during multiplication correction. The operation of this chassis is described in section 5.6.

If $2^0 R_2 = 1$, what must be done is as follows:

(1) Prevent an end of operation signal from going to the control,

(2) Put a subtract order into R_4,

(3) Perform the subtraction,

(4) Change $2^0 R_2$ to 0.

These operations are initiated on the recognition signal for multiplication, the sensing being done in C49 and C61. The multiplication correction toggle C62, which has been in the 1 state, is turned to 0. (It should be noted here that the recognition signal comes very shortly after YGR^2 and that there are still two operations left, namely YC and BG. Thus there is ample time for the turnover of the necessary flipflop. This inhibits the "end of

131

operation" signal in M20 and M9. It also operates the gates C53, and C65 which change "multiply" to "subtract" by turning flipflops D63 and D69.

A turnover signal from M8 via gate B10 then flips false control flipflop B4 and initiates the sequence necessary to start the subtract operation. (See Section 5.6).

The subtraction is carried out in the usual way, and on YGR^1 and add C51 is enabled. This operates gate tube C50b and turns $2^0 R_2$ to 0. The turning of $2^0 R_2$ to 0, by inverter C50a and gate C63, turns flipflop C62 back to 1, and this permits the "end of operation" signal to go through.

<u>Left and Right Shift</u> The operations of left shift and right shift are so designed as to produce algebraically correct shifts in R_1. This is done on a left shift by not shifting the sign digit. On a right shift the sign digit is shifted and the sign is held fixed. Thus the same circuit used in multiplication can be used, and this circuit is used in all operations involving a right shift. There is no difficulty in addition since the contents of $2^0 R_1$ are lost on the left shift. The left shift and right shift orders send a "0" signal to the Shift Sequencing Chassis via the <u>OR</u> circuits C45 and C20.

On a right shift, as described in Section 5.9, the overflow from $2^{-39} R_2$ is lost.

On a left shift the overflow from $2^{-1} R_1$ goes into $2^{39} R_2$, all of R_{II} shifts, and the overflow from $2^0 R_2$ is lost. The shift into $2^0 R_2$ from $2^0 R_1$ is taken care of by J12, which operates the red gate from 2^0R^1 to 2^0R_2 on the signals divide, left shift, print, or input. At the same time "0" is put into $2^{-39}R_1$, by J9 and J10 as explained under addition and subtraction.

The shift into $2^{-39}R_2$ from $2^{-1}R_1$ is made by J2 and J6. On the left shift order the cathode of J2 operates gate J6 on RGR_1 and gates $2^{-1}R^1$ into $2^{-39}R_2$. On all other orders the usual red gate from $2^{-1}R^1$ into 2^0R_2 operates, and this gate is controlled by J5. The gate works on RGR_1 and a "not left shift" signal from J11.

Division. Restoring division is used (See Chapter 1). The quotient is formed in 39 steps, the quotient digits being inserted one at a time into the right hand end of R_2 and shifted left.

Three signs must be sensed. We sense the signs of:

(1) Divisor, which is in R^3,

(2) Dividend, which is in R^1,

(3) Tentative partial remainder, which is in the digit resolver.

The rules are as follows:

(1) If signs of divisor and dividend

        (a) Agree, subtract throughout process

        (b) Disagree, add throughout process

(2) If signs of tentative partial remainder and dividend

        (a) Agree, accept TPR, using RC, GG, YC, BG

        (b) Disagree, reject TPR, using BC, YG, YC, BG

(3) If signs of TPR and divisor

(a) <u>Agree, insert</u> 1 as quotient digit

(b) <u>Disagree, insert</u> 0 as quotient digit

The sign of the dividend is soon lost so it must be stored. It is stored by gating it into D63, the $\pm$ flipflop in such a way as to set the complement gate for the division. This gating is done by GGR^3, the gate which brings the divisor in from the memory and is described in the discussion of the Interplay Control. Since D64, the Number-Absolute Value flipflop has previously been set to 1 as one of the digits of the divide order, then the complement gate will be set for <u>add</u> or <u>subtract</u> according as $2^0 R^3$ is 0 or 1. (See Addition and Subtraction).

The sign of the tentative partial remainder is sensed by J21 and the signals TPR+ and TPR- are supplied to C60 and C58, respectively. These tubes, with signals from D63 via D51, test agreement or disagreement of TPR and dividend. If there is agreement, C59 goes negative, causing a signal "1" via the chain C69, C57, C8. If there is disagreement, inverter C56 goes negative and a signal "0" is supplied via C68, C57 and C20. The tube C70 is a check that the complement gate is set correctly. It should be pointed out here that before the end of the carry delay the tentative partial remainder may have a different sign from the one it finally assumes in R^1. This causes no difficulty since the correct clear will occur later and permit the proper gate to follow.

Signals TPR+ and TPR- also go to C72 and C58 where they are

compared with $2^0 R^3$. If they disagree the OR circuit C71 goes negative and this signal goes to J19. If they agree, the output of J19 is positive and does nothing. Meanwhile, $2^{-39}R_2$ is being held to 1 by J20, so that on the YGR^2 a 1 is gated to $2^{-39}R^2$ and then to $2^{-38}R_2$ by RGR_2. That is, a 1 is introduced and shifted left.

If there is a disagreement, conduction through the diode J17 holds $2^{-39}R^2$ to a 0 during the YGR^2 and a 0 is thus put into $2^{-38}R_2$ on RGR_2.

Holding $2^{-39}R_2$ to 1 leaves it this way at the end of the division, which is desired for the division roundoff.

Division is stopped exactly like multiplication, a pair of signals having gone to the shift counter on each YGR_2 and RGR_2.

OP Turnover Enable Signal. This signal permits the change from control to operate. If the End and Reset flipflops B6 and B14 are both set to zero, then B24b is positive and C64b is negative. Moreover, if the R_4 gate has acted, C66 has been set to 1, making C47b negative. This creates the OP Turnover Enable.

135

5.10 <u>Auxiliary Chassis</u> - <u>Clear Driver Drivers</u>. These chassis of which there are 3, have the function of supplying signals to the clear drivers, and their reason for being is simply to supply fast moving signals. They are 6-tube chassis, and 1 1/2 5687's are allocated to each clear.

A. Clear Driver Driver R_I. This chassis has 4 inputs marked Red, Black, Yellow and Green which come from A6a, A6b, A36b and A36a, respectively. The four outputs go to the four corresponding clear drivers of R_I.

Each input has a bleeder attached to hold the input up when the connection to the shift sequencing chassis is removed. This was put in primarily for convenience in installation.

B. Clear Driver Driver R_{II}. Since RCR^2 is never used, only 4 1/2 tubes are needed for the three clears in R_{II}. However, it is necessary to GCR_2 both for the usual down left gate and for the R order. Therefore one of the unused tubes is used as an "or" circuit for the two GCR_2 signals. One of these signals comes from GCR_1 cathode in the usual slave fashion. The other comes from P14 (See Drawings 301 and 288) via tube 1 in the R_{III} gate driver. This last tube is being used to supply a clear voltage and is available because there is no BGR_3.

The other two inputs to this chassis come from F10 to furnish BCR^2 and from H6 to furnish YCR_2.

The three outputs of the clear driver driver R_{II} chassis go to the corresponding three R_{II} clear drivers.

136

C. Clear Driver Driver R_{III}. No YCR_3 is used, so that only 3 inputs to this chassis are needed. They are labeled R, B and G and come from P2a, P2b, and P1a of the register selection chassis. The three outputs go to the corresponding three R_{III} clear drivers.

Complement Gate Drivers (Drawing 198). There are two complement gate drivers which work in push pull. Their functions are to receive inputs from the control at flipflop voltage levels (0v or 029v) and to deliver voltages of +90v or -30v to the grids of the complement gate. One of the two complement gate driver chassis is supplied with a bleeder on the input so that the complement gate will be in the ADD state if no signal is supplied to the drivers.

Inputs to the complement gate drivers are from C30 and C41 in the arithmetic control.

Odd and Even Order Gate Chassis (Drawing 250, 251). These chassis transfer the instruction part of an order from R_3 to R_4. The gates are double gates so that no clearing of R_4 is necessary. Signals for gating come from M25 and M26 and are discussed in the interplay control.

Odd Address Gate Chassis (Drawing 249). All addresses are sensed from the even address flipflops. Therefore when the odd order is gated to R_4, the odd address is gated at the same time to the even address flipflops. This chassis is identical to the two described above.

Even Address Cathode Follower Chassis (Drawing 252).
This chassis has two functions:

(1) On signal from M72 it gates the contents of
the even address flipflops to the dispatch counter,

(2) It has cathode followers from which the even
address signals to the address generator and to the recognition
circuit are taken.

Driver III Chassis (Drawing 171). The principal function
of this chassis is to furnish the "or" circuits necessary for the
slaving of R_{II} to R_I. Its role in the logic of shifting is important, and in Drawing 189 the lower 7 boxes refer to the Driver
III chassis.

Counter Output Chassis. (Drawing 253). This chassis has
two functions:

(1) It furnishes cathode follower outputs for the
six stages of the shift counter which go to the recognition circuit,

(2) It contains the logical circuit which inhibits
YCR_2 when YCR_1 is ordered specifically in an order. This circuit
is made up of H4b and H6.

End Connections . (Drawings 257 and 273). Because of the
different requirement of the orders executed by ORDVAC, a considerable
amount of switching of the end and near-end digits of the registers
is needed. The circuits for carrying out this switching have been
located in small chassis near the ends of the registers, the locations

138

being shown on the right side of Drawing 273. For convenience in reference, the tubes in these chassis have been numbered serially from 1 to 25 and are referred to as Chassis J.

The operations carried out by Chassis J are shown in Drawing 257:

A. Gates 0 into $2^{-39}R_1$ on every RGR_2 except the RGR_2 of the add order. In this case $2^{-1} R^2$ is gated to $2^{-39} R_1$. This is carried out by J9 and J10a.

B. Gates $2^{-1} R^2$ into $2^{0}R_2$ on divide, left shift, print or input and RGR_2. This is a double gate because $2^{0}R_2$ is not cleared by GCR_2. The tubes used are J12 and the upper gate tube in the $2^{0}R_{II}$ column. .

C. On a left shift order the sign digit of R_1 must be preserved and appropriate gating must be arranged. The flipflop $2^{0}R^2$ is used to store the contents of $2^{0}R_1$. On YGR^1 or GGR^1 gate tube J3 always gates $2^{0}R_1$ to $2^{0}R^2$. If there is a left shift order, then on RGR_1 we gate $2^{0}R^2$ back to $2^{0}R_1$. This is done with "and" circuit J2 using the lower gate in $2^{-1} R_I$. At the same time, using gate J6a we gate $2^{-1}R^1$ to $2^{-39}R_2$.

If there is no left shift order, then via "not" J11b and "and" J5 we gate $2^{-1}R^1$ to $2^{0}R_1$ on RGR_1.

D. On every BGR_1 the contents of $2^{-39}R^1$ go to $2^{-1}R_2$. The gate tube is J10b and the signal from $2^{-39}R^1$ comes via cathode follower J6b.

E. The digit resolver signals for division are obtained

139

from the most significant stage. For the push-pull output
needed it is inverted in J22a with J22b acting as cathode follower.
The other signal is from cathode follower J21b.

F. This circuit, using tubes J15 through J20 has
several functions. It furnishes signals for inserting the proper
quotient digit into R_2 and it preserves R_2 on the A and add orders.

On every BGR_2 we gate $2^{-39} R_2$ into the flipflop J16 using
the upper gate tube in the $2^{-39}R_{II}$ column. If there is an add or
A order then J18 causes gate J17a to gate J16 to $2^{-39} R_2$ on RGR_2.

The divide order will cause J20b to conduct and hold $2^{-39} R_2$
to 1. If TPR and divisor disagree, J19 goes negative and the diode
J17b inhibits YGR^2. Since BCR^2 made $2^{-39}R^2 = 0$, this puts in a zero.
Otherwise a 1 goes in.

The holding to 1 of $2^{-39}R_2$ also furnishes the division
roundoff.

G. This circuit is associated with input-output and
is also shown on Drawing 271. The flipflop "CH. I TOG" is shown
in Drawing 326. Operation of this circuit is described in Section 3.3.

140

PART II

THE INTERPLAY CONTROL. The circuits of the memory synchronization chassis (Drawing 290), the register selection chassis
(Drawing 288), and the memory control chassis (Drawing 289) are
rather closely inter-related and are called the interplay control.
(Drawing 301). The primary functions of the interplay control
are to do the following things:

(1) Supervise the transfer of order pairs from the
memory to the order register, the gating of instructions to the
decoding register, and address gating;

(2) Supervise the execution of orders involving
transfer of control;

(3) Synchronize the control with the memory;

(4) Perform further decoding of decoding chassis
outputs to provide required signals to the memory (both reading
and writing);

(5) Supervise clearing and gating for arithmetic
operations executed in synchronism with the memory;

(6) Supervise clearing and gating in the dispatch
counter (also executed in synchronism with the memory);

(7) Perform further decoding of decoding chassis
outputs to provide initiating signals for the arithmetic stop
chassis;

(8) Provide and combine completion signals for
orders.

141

5.11 <u>Handling of Orders and Instructions</u>. Orders are generally stored in the memory in pairs in successive memory locations. The sequence of steps followed in executing a series of orders, if none of the orders is a control transfer order, is listed below:

(a) The order pair is transferred from the memory location indicated by the control counter into the order Register R_3. During this process, the number in the control counter is increased by one;

(b) The digits 0-9 of the order register are gated by the even order gate into the decoding register R_4.

(c) The even order (left order of the order pair) is executed;

(d) The digits 20-29 of the order register are gated by the odd order gate into the decoding register. The digits 30-39 of the order register are gated by the odd address gate to digits 10-19 of the order register;

(e) The odd order (right hand order of the order pair) is executed;

(f) Steps (a) through (e) are repeated. Note that the memory address consulted has been increased by one.

<u>Detailed Description of Circuits</u>. The circuits used primarily for the handling of orders include the A, B, and C flipflops (N13, 14, 15) of the memory synchronization chassis with their associated gating, inverting, and cathode follower circuits

142

(N1-3, 7-9, 19-22, 26b, 27, 31a, 32). Also included are "AND" circuits (N25, 26a, 33, 34a, M1, 2, 14), gate driver circuits (M13, 25, 26) and gate sensing logical circuits (M40, 41).

The C flipflop (N15), also called the control-operate flipflop, is in the 0 or operate state during the execution of an order, and is in the 1 or control state while transfers of instructions or orders are being executed. This flipflop thus serves to distinguish between so-called "operate" sequences, during which orders are executed, and "control" sequences, during which the orders are transferred. The A and B flipflops (N13, 14) are used for sequencing purposes while orders are being transferred. The information that the even (or odd) order is to be next executed is retained by the A and B flipflops during the execution of orders.

The operation of the circuits will be described under the assumption that no transfer of control occurs. In particular, the lead "(not $\bar{C}'$)" (M38, N1, 8) is negative and the lead "$\bar{C}$ v $\bar{C}'$ (op)" (M29 N3) is positive. For discussion purposes, the flip-flops are assumed to be initially in the states A = 0, B = 1, C = 1. (See Table 5.6). All grids of "and" circuit 33, 34a are negative and the negative cathodes provide a "use memory" stimulus and enable clearing and gating pulses from the memory to execute the transfer of an order pair to the order register. During this time, memory pulses are used to increase the address in the order counter by one. (See Section 5.16). After the order pair has been

transferred, the cathode of tube N8 is pulled negative.   The
grid (pin 6) of tube N8a is positive by virtue of the fact that
the input (not $\bar{C}'$) to inverter N1 is negative.   Triode N8a conducts and flipflop B is thereby set to 0.

FLIPFLOP

A	B	C	Corresponding Operation
0	1	1	Transfer of Order Pair from Memory to R_3
0	0	1	Even Order Gate
0	0	0	Interim State
1	0	0	Execution of Even Order
1	0	1	Interim State
1	1	1	Odd Order Gate, Odd Address Gate
1	1	0	Interim State
0	1	0	Execution of Odd Order

Table 5.6

Sequence of States of A, B and C Flipflops

The state A = 0, B = 0, C = 1 then enables the even order gates
through "and" circuit M1, 14a, and through circuits M31b and
M26. The even order gate, odd order gate, and odd address gate
are sensed (tubes M40, 41) to produce a signal, called the R_4
gate, which is negative if the even order gate is negative, or
if both the odd order gate and odd address gate are negative.
When the R_4 gate signal and the "Op turnover enable" (C52 P21)
signal are both negative, the cathode of "and" circuit P21 will

144

be negative. (Conditions under which "Op turnover enable", C52, P21, is negative are discussed in Section 5.9). As a result the cathode of gate N9a will be pulled negative. Since the grid (pin 3) of N9a is positive (See Section 5.18), the flipflop N15 will be set to the operate or O state.

At this time the state of the flipflops is A = 0, B = 0, C = 0. When the C flipflop N15 is turned to 0, the execution of the instruction just transferred to the decoding register is begun. Simultaneously, the cathode of gate N7 is pulled negative through N21a, N22a, and N27, so that the A flipflop N13 is set to disagree with the B flipflop N14. In this case the B flipflop is 0, so that grids of N21b and of N7b are positive, and the A flipflop N13 is set to 1. When the execution of the even order is completed, the operate-control flipflop N15 is again set to the control, or 1 state.

Corresponding to the state A = 1, B = 0, C = 1, the three grids of the "and" circuit N25, 26a, are negative, resulting in the setting of the B flipflop N14 to the 1 state. In the process the 0 state of the B flipflop is sensed to produce a signal which sets the B flipflop to the state. For stability, the pair of inverters of N32 has been added. To prevent incorrect gating by N7a, the positive excursion of the output voltage of the second inverter N32b is limited to approximately Ov, by the diode connected clamp N31a.

At this time the flipflops are in the state A = 1, B = 1,

145

C = 1, with the result that the cathode of "and" circuit M2, 14b is negative. Gating voltages for the odd order gate (Drawing 250) and for the odd address gate (Drawing 249) are then supplied by the action of M13a, and M25. The odd order gate transfers the odd instruction from digits 20-29 of the order register to the decoding register. The odd address gate transfers the odd address from digits 30-39 of the order register to digits 10-19 of the order register. Both the odd order gate and odd address gate are sensed by "and" circuit M41 in order that an R_4 gate signal may be produced. The R_4 gate signal indirectly results in setting flipflop N15 to the 0 or operate state. As the execution of the odd order begins, concurrently the A flipflop N13 is set to disagree with the B flipflop N14. Completion of the odd order results in the setting of the flipflop N15 to the 1 or control state and the flipflops are in the original state A = 0, B = 1, C = 1.

5.12 TRANSFER OF CONTROL. As discussed in Section 5.11, order pairs generally stored in successive memory locations. It is essential that provision be made for departing from the normal sequence of executing orders; i.e., some method of transferring control must be provided. In ORDVAC, four control transfer orders U, U', C, C' are provided; furthermore, transfer of control is effected during the execution of the A and conditional stop orders. For the four control transfer orders U, U', C, C' provision is made for transferring to either order of the order pair. The un-primed orders (U, C) transfer control to the left hand (even) order; the primed orders (U', C') transfer to the right hand (odd) orders. Of the four transfer orders U, U', C, C', two (C, C') are conditional; that is, a transfer of control is executed only if the sign digit of the accumulator is a zero.

The transfer of control of the U, U', C, C' order is handled quite differently from the transfer of control which occurs during the execution of the A or stop orders. It is therefore convenient to describe the two transfer of control processes separately.

The technique of executing the control transfer orders is best described as a departure from the normal routine as dis-cussed in Section 5.11. It should be recalled that at the time of the completion of the right hand (odd) order of the order pair the control counter holds the address of the next order pair to be executed. Furthermore, the A and B flipflops N13, 14 of the memory synchronization chassis indicate that the step to be taken after the completion of the odd order is the transfer of the next order pair from the memory. If a transfer of control is to be made for execution of one of the U, U', C, C' orders, it is necessary to gate the control transfer address to the control counter and to indicate (perhaps falsely) that the odd order has been completed. In this way it is assured that the next step will be the transfer of the desired order pair from the memory.

147

One further departure from the normal sequence is necessary for the transfer of control of the U' and C' orders. Ordinarily the transfer of the order pair from the memory is followed by the gating of the even instruction to the decoding register; for the U' and C' orders the order pair transfer should be followed by the gating of the odd instruction to the decoding register and of the odd address to the even address. In the ORDVAC, the decoding register and the sign digit of the accumulator are sensed to control the gating of the A and B flipflops N13, 14 to change the normal sequence.

In the transfer of control occurring in the A and conditional stop orders, the normal sequence of the A, B, and C flipflops N13, 14, 15 is left unchanged. The transfer of control is effected by gating the address portion of the A or stop order to the control counter as a preliminary step in the execution of the order.

Detailed Description of Control Transfer Orders. Logical circuitry in the interplay control (Drawings 301, 288, 289, 290) used in the execution of control transfer orders includes tubes M37a, 37b, 38a, 39 and 29. Special gating of the A and B flipflops N13, 14 is accomplished by use of M3 and M8b. The circuits of M30 and M17b are associated with the stop order. The signal used for gating the address to the control counter is called "false use memory" and is formed by the circuits of M17a, 18, M46 and M35a.

In the decoding chassis (refer to Section 5.8), the decoding register and the sign digit of R_1 are sensed and the signals $\bar{C}$ (D18, M37) and $\bar{C}$· (D15, M37) are generated. The signal $\bar{C}$ is negative under two conditions:

(1) The instruction U is held in the decoding register;

(2) The instruction C is held in the decoding register and the sign digit of the accumulator is 0. The signal $\bar{C}$ is negative under similar conditions for the U' and C' orders.

If a transfer of control is to be executed, one of the signals $\bar{C}$ or $\bar{C}$· will go negative when the control transfer order is gated to the decoding register. By action of one of the inverters of M37, one of the grids of M39 is positive, with the result that the grid (pin 6) of M29 is negative. The turnover of the control-operate flipflop N15 to the operate or 0 state then causes the other grid (pin 5) of "and" circuit M29 to go negative, thereby causing plate current to flow in gate tube N3a. The B flipflop may have been in either the 0 or 1 state; the action of M29 and gate N3 guarantees that N14 is now in the 1 state. Gate N7 sets the A flipflop N13 to the opposite state from·the B flipflop; it is thus assured that the A flipflop is now in the 0 state. The negative cathode of "and" circuit M29 also simulates "or" circuit M17a, 18b. The other inputs to "or" circuit M17a, 18b are negative during execution of the A and stop orders, respective-

ly; they are positive at this time. The negative output of
"or" circuit M17a, 18b is sensed by inverter 46a and produces a
positive voltage at the cathode (pin 7) of M35a. This positive
signal is called the "false use memory" signal. The "false
use memory" signal commands that the memory be synchronized with
the control and is also used to control memory pulses for the
gating of the order address to the control counter. The techniques by which control and memory are synchronized are discussed in Section 5.13; control counter gating is discussed in
Section 5.16. Completion of the action cycle enables the turnover of the control-operate flipflop N15 to the control or 1
state. At this time the control counter contains the address
part of the control transfer order, the A flipflop is in the 0
state, and the B flipflop is in the 1 state. The turnover of the
control-operate flipflop to the control state enables an action
cycle which transfers the desired order pair to the order register R_3. Completion of the action cycle produces a negative
voltage on the grid (pin 5) of N2 and on the cathode of gate tube
N8. It should be recalled that the control transfer order remains
in the decoding register so that either $\bar{C}$ (D18 M37) or $\bar{C}'$ (D15
M37) is negative. If the control transfer order is an unprimed
order $\bar{C}$ will be negative, (not $\bar{C}'$) (M38 N1, 8) will be negative,
the grid (pin 6) of gate tube N8a will be positive and the B
flipflop N14 will be set to 0. The normal sequence of even order

then follows. On the other hand, if the control transfer order
was one of the primed orders U' or C' the lead $\bar{C}$ (D18, M37) is
negative and lead (not $\bar{C}'$) (M38 N1, 8) is positive. The grid
(pin 5) of 8b is positive and the A flipflop N13 is set to the
1 state. The transfer of the order pair to the order register
R_3 is in this case followed by the odd order gate and odd address
gate and by the execution of the odd order.

Notice that the sensing of the decoding chassis by way
of $\bar{C}'$ (D18 M37) and (not $\bar{C}'$) (M38 N1, 8) for gating of the A
and B flipflops is exceptional. In this case, the decoding
chassis is sensed while the control-operate flipflop N15 is in
the control state. For all other outputs of the decoding chassis
it is required that the control-operate flipflop be in the operate
state before execution of any step of an order can occur.

Detailed Description of Transfer of Control in Stop and
A Orders. In the decoding chassis the decoding register and the
control-operate flipflop are sensed and the signals $\begin{bmatrix} A\ (Op) \end{bmatrix}$
(D41, M18, 19, 45, P8) and $\begin{bmatrix} Stop\ (Op) \end{bmatrix}$ (D40 M17) are generated.
If the control-operate flipflop N15 is in the operate or 0
state and if one of the instructions A or Stop is in the de-
coding register, the corresponding signal $\begin{bmatrix} A\ (Op)\ or\ Stop\ (op) \end{bmatrix}$
will be negative. In either case one of the inputs to "or"
circuit M17a, 18b will be negative, the stop (Op) signal is
inverted twice by "not" circuits M17b, M30a, and is then used.

151

as an input to "or" circuit M17a, 18b through the cathode follower M30b. The output of "or" circuit M17a, 18b is inverted by
M46a, the positive excursion is limited by M46b, and the signal
is fed through cathode follower M35a, to become the "false use
memory" signal. When the false use memory signal becomes positive,
a memory action cycle is enabled and the address is transferred
from the order register R_3 to the control counter. After the
action cycle, the "have used memory" and "have gated to order
register" signals (See Sections 5.13 and 5.16) initiate the remaining steps for the A order and serve as a completion signal
for the Stop order.

5.13 Synchronization of Control with Memory. The
memory of the ORDVAC is synchronously operated at a basic re-
petition rate of 24 μ sec. The controlling pulses of the memory
of interest in this section (refer to Drawing 333) are listed
below in the time sequence in which they occur:

(1)	Writing Dash pulse	3.6 μ sec.
(2)	Dash End pulse	2.2 μ sec.
(3)	Action Sense pulse	2.5 μ sec.
(4)	Delay pulse	2.5 μ sec.
(5)	Up counter pulse	5.0 μ sec.

With the exception of the writing dash pulse, which overlaps
the dash end pulse somewhat, the end of each of the above pulses
triggers the beginning of the next. The remainder of the 24 μ
sec. period -- approximately 9 μ sec. -- is dead time. Ordinarily

the memory and the control operate independently; the memory
during periods of this sort regenerates words at successive
addresses -- one word for each 24 μ sec. period. (In this case,
the 24 μ sec. period is called a regeneration cycle). The control, meanwhile operates asynchronously. When it becomes necessary for the memory to communicate with the control or arithmetic unit, the control and the memory must be synchronized for
a single 24 μ sec. period, called an action cycle. The communication takes the form of reading, (transferring 40 digit words
from the memory to one of the registers) or of writing (transferring a word from the accumulator register R_2 to the memory).

The synchronization is effected in the following manner.
The control manufactures a "memory enable" signal, which may
occur at any time during the fundamental 24 μ sec. period. When
the "memory enable" signal and one of the memory pulses, namely
the action sense pulse, are coincident in time, the signal is
normally given to the memory that an action cycle is to begin.
The "memory enable" signal is longer than the action cycle, since
it is negative not only during the action cycle, but also during
any waiting period preceding the action sense pulse. During the
action cycle the clearing and gating processes necessary for the
transfer of a word to or from the memory are executed more or
less directly by the memory pulses. During the next action sense
pulse, 24 μ sec. after the beginning of the action cycle, the
"have used memory" signal is given to the control to indicate

153

that the word transfer is complete, and the control resumes asynchronous operation.

Two flipflops are necessary for the synchronization process. One, the action-regenerate flipflop, normally serves to distinguish between an actional cycle and a regeneration cycle. The second, the synchronization flipflop, is necessary to differentiate between the period of time before the action cycle and the period during which the "have used memory" signal is present. An interruption in the "memory enable" signal after the action cycle has been completed is used for the resetting of the synchronization flipflop.

Detailed Description. The circuits used for synchronization of the control with the memory include the action-regenerate flipflop N17, the synchronization flipflop N18, their associated gates and cathode followers N4, 11, 12, 24a and the circuits of N6, N29 and N34b.

Initially, the "memory enable" signal, i.e., the cathode (pin 8) of N35b, is positive and the memory is regenerating; the action-regenerate flipflop N17 is in the regenerate or 1 state. The grid (pin 3) of N12a is positive and the synchronization flipflop N18 is held in the 0 state as long as the "memory enable" signal is positive. When communication with the memory is desired, the "memory enable" signal goes negative (See Section 14), leaving the synchronization flipflop N18 in the 0 state. Both grids of "and-not" circuit N29 are negative; the output is therefore positive.

The positive excursion of the output of N29 is limited to 0v
by the diode action of N34b to prevent spurious gating by gate
N11a when the action sense pulse is not present. The action
sense pulse, like all pulses listed above is a 20v. negative
pulse, the voltage ranging from -10v. during the pulse to +10v.
when the pulse is not present. With the grid of gate 11a at
0v., the action sense pulse sets the action-regenerate flipflop
N17 to the action or 0 state. The grid (pin 7) of gate N12b is
positive, so that the writing dash pulse sets the synchronization
flipflop N18 to the 1 state. The turnover of the synchronization
flipflop disables gate N11a and enables gate N11b, so that when
the next action sense pulse pulls the cathode of N11 negative,
the action-regenerate flipflop N17 is returned to the regenerate
or 1 state. Both grids of "and" circuit N6 are now negative and
the negative cathode provides the "have used memory" signal to
the control. Before another action cycle can occur, it is
necessary that the "memory enable" signal go positive in order
that the synchronization flipflop will be reset to the 0 state.
Although it is possible for two action cycles to occur successively if the "memory enable" signal is interrupted for a period of
time shorter than the action sense pulse, in practice an action
cycle is always followed by at least one regeneration cycle.

    5.14 MEMORY SIGNALS PROVIDED BY INTERPLAY CONTROL.
Logical circuits are provided in the interplay control to provide the following signals associated with use of the memory:

(1) The "memory enable" signal;

(2) Signals directing the address generator to
consult addresses indicated either in R_3 or in the dispatch
counter;

(3) Regenerate or Read (R) signals to individual
memory chassis;

(4) Action and Write (W) signals to individual
memory chassis.

Various combinations of these signals are enabled, depending
upon the particular manner in which the memory is being employed.
Utilization of the memory in synchronism with the control assumes
one of the following forms:

(1) Transfer of order pairs from the memory to the
order register R_3;

(2) Transfer of numbers from the memory to the
number register R^3 or to the arithmetic register R_2;

(3) Transfer of words or parts of words from the
accumulator R_1 into the memory;

(4) Utilization of memory pulses for synchronous
gating of addresses to the order counter during transfer of control and for transfer of numbers from the arithmetic register R_2
to the number register R^3 during the A order.

In all cases a "memory enable" signal must first be
provided in order that synchronization of memory and control can·
be effected. Any one of three signals will provide the "memory
enable" stimulus: first, the fact that the A, B, and C flipflops

156

are in the state A = 0, B = 1, and C = 1 for reading out order pairs to R_3; second, a "true use memory" signal from the decoding chassis for either reading or writing of words or parts thereof as part of the execution of an order; or third, a "false use memory" signal for gating an address to the control counter during a transfer of control and for gating to the number register R^3 preliminary to the A order.

The address generator in the memory must be provided with addresses under three conditions. During regeneration cycles, the address of the regeneration counter must be supplied to the address generator. For transfer of order pairs to the order register R_3, the address generator must be supplied with the address in the control counter during the action cycle. For communication between the memory and the arithmetic unit during execution of orders, the address generator must be supplied with the address part of the order in the order register R_3. The regeneration counter and the control counter have been combined to form the dispatch counter (Section 5.16) and have what is called the dispatch register of ten flipflops in common. Counting operations are programmed in such a way that address sensing by the address generator is done while either the regeneration address or the control address is in the dispatch register. The address generator has been constructed with facilities for switching between two address inputs; namely, the dispatch register of the dispatch counter and the address in the order register R_3. During execution of orders

157

involving the "true use memory" enabling signal, the address
generator is instructed to sense the address part of the order
in the order register R_3. During execution of orders involving
the "false use memory" enabling signal, instructions are given
to the dispatch counter and to the memory so that the regeneration continues without interruption.

Signals must also be generated for each of the forty
memory chassis. In reading or in regenerating, each digit of
the word is sensed and regenerated in the corresponding memory
chassis. In writing, digits are sensed in the accumulator and
are written into the memory. Digits are written in either blocks
of ten for the E and E' orders or in blocks of forty for the M
order. Three signals are provided in the interplay control for
writing purposes; WE for digits 10-19, WE' for digits 30-39 and
W for the remaining twenty digits (0-9 and 20-29). All three
signals are negative during the action cycle in the execution of
the M order.

Formation of "Memory Enable" Signal. The logical circuits
involved in the formation of the "memory enable" signal (cathode
of N35b) are associated with tubes M17a, 18, 46, 35a, 3b, 21, 10
and N28, 35. The "memory enable" signal is negative under three
conditions: (1) state A = 0, B = 1, C = 1 of the flipflops N13,
14, 15 sensed at the cathode of "and" circuit N33, 34a; (2) "true
use memory" (D55, M3) formed in the decoding chassis; or (3)
"false use memory" sensed at the output of "or" circuit M17a, 18.

The inputs to "or" circuit M17a, 18 are A (Op), (D41 M18);
Stop (Op) and $\bar{C}$ v $\bar{C}'$ (Op). The "true use memory" and "false
use memory" signals are inverted (M⁴6a and M3b) and used as
inputs to "and-not" circuit M21. The output of M21 is negative
for either of the two "use memory" signals and is called "op.
mem. enable". The "op. mem. enable" signal is an input to "and"
circuit N28; the other input to N28 is negative when "op. mem.
enable" first goes negative. The "memory enable" signal will
be negative if either the cathode of N28 or the cathode of N33,
34a is negative, by the action of "or" circuit N35.

Formation of Address Generator Signals. The circuits
associated with tubes P5 and P6 are used to form the signals to
the address generator. The address generator senses the address
digits 10-19 of the order register R_3 during an action cycle if
the "true use memory" signal is negative; otherwise the dispatch
register of the dispatch counter is sensed. "Action" and "true
use memory" are inputs to "and" circuit P5, the output of P5
is "address generator read R_3". The output of P5 is inverted in
P6 to form "address generator reads counter".

Formation of Signals for Memory Chassis. The signals
"regenerate or read" and "action and write" used in the memory
chassis are generated in the circuits of D37, 38 and M4, 5, 6,
15, 16, 27 and 38b. Writing into the memory occurs only during
execution of the M, E, and E' orders. The corresponding signal,
called "use memory, write (op)" (D31 M27) is generated in the

159

decoding chassis. The "action and write" signal is negative during the action cycle occurring as a part of the execution of the M, E, and E' orders, otherwise the "regenerate or read" signal is negative. The "use memory, write (op)" signal and the "action" signal are applied as input to "and-not" circuit M27. The output of M27 and of cathode follower M38b is therefore positive only during the action cycle occurring during execution of the M, E, or E' orders and is negative during regeneration or reading cycles. The cathode of M38b provides the "regenerate or read" signals to all memory chassis.

The generation of the "action and write" signals for the memory chassis is more complicated. Three separate "action and write" signals are provided as follows:

(1) The W signal provides "action and write" signals to chassis 0-9 and 20-29 and is negative during the action cycle of the M order.

(2) The WE signal provides "action and write" signals to chassis 10-19 and is negative during the action cycle of either the M order or of the E' order.

(3) The WE' signal provides "action and write" signals to chassis 30-39 and is negative during the action cycle of either the M order or of the E order. The W, WE, and WE' signals are generated as positive signals and are inverted by "not" circuits M6b, 4a, and 4b respectively. The generation of the three "action and write" signals may be a source of confusion for two reasons:

160

(1) Positive signals rather than negative signals are the actuating signals in the logical circuitry. The result is that in logical drawings, opposite grids of flipflops are sensed and "or" circuits become "and" circuits, and vice versa.

(2) An identity of Boolean algebra is used to simplify the circuitry. The identity is x' $vxy = x'vy$ where the symbol v represents "or", x' is "not x," and xy is "x and y". In this case x is a binary variable representing the A. V. flip-flop D64 and y represents the +, - flipflop D63.

States of decoding register flipflops used to indicate the M, E and E' instructions are shown in the function register order code, Drawing 307. The logical equivalent (for positive actuating signals) of the circuitry generating the three "action and write" signals is shown in Figure 5.6. Note that the cathode of D38 is positive if either the M instruction or the E instruction is in the decoding register, but not if the E' instruction is being sensed. The D37 cathode is similarly positive for the M or E' instructions, but not for the E instruction.

One final comment should be made with regard to the design of circuits supplying the "action and write" signals to the memory chassis. Each chassis contains a 1 ma. bleeder designed to increase the input voltage by approximately ten volts. (See Drawing 196, tube W11). The bleeders must be considered in the selection of the cathode resistors of the cathode followers M15, 16. As an example, the equivalent circuit for the AE cathode

161

follower M15a is shown in Figure 5.7. If M15a did not conduct, the cathode voltage would fall to approximately -70v. In order that the cathode voltage may rise to 0v, M15a must conduct 14 ma; 11 ma will then flow through the bleeders in the memory chassis, and a current of 25 ma flows through the cathode resistors.

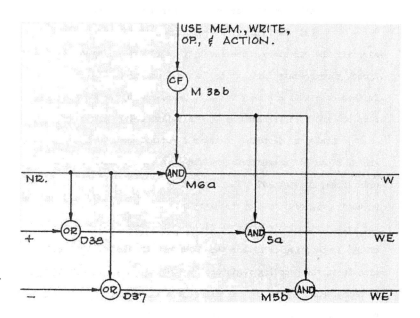

FIGURE 5.6

Formation of Write Signals for Memory Chassis

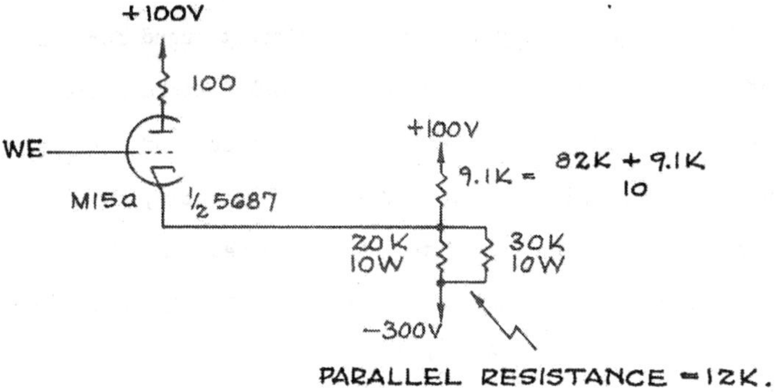

+100V

100

WE

M15a ½ 5687

+100V

9.1K = 82K + 9.1K / 10

20K 10W   30K 10W

−300V

PARALLEL RESISTANCE = 12K.

Cathode Follower Circuit for WE Signal

FIGURE 5.7

5.15 CLEARING AND GATING FOR WORD TRANSFERS EXECUTED

IN SYNCHRONISM WITH THE MEMORY.   Word transfers from the memory

to the registers of the arithmetic unit or control are executed

in synchronism with pulses of the memory. The number transfer

from the arithmetic register R_2 to the number register R_3 which

is part of the A order is also executed in synchronism with the

memory pulses. The complete list of clears and gates executed

in synchronism with the memory is given in Table 5.7 above.

In all cases clearing occurs during the up counter pulse time and gating occurs during the writing dash pulse time. Circuits are provided to check that the clearing and gating voltages have gone negative. The checking circuits provide a "have cleared and gated" signal which must be present if any further steps are to be executed.

Detailed Description. The circuits used for generation of clearing and gating voltages for word transfers executed in synchronism with the memory comprise the bulk of the register selection chassis (Drawing 288). In particular, the tubes used are P1b, 2, 3, 4b, and P7 to P20 inclusive. The checking circuits are found in the memory control chassis, Drawing 289. Tubes M49a, 50-54, 61, 62, 64b, and 65-68 are used for this purpose.

Since the four clearing and gating sequences listed in Table 5.6 are quite similar, only one -- the transfer of a number from the memory to the number register R^3 -- will be described in detail.

It is assumed that one of the arithmetic orders (addition, multiplication or division) has been gated to the decoding register. The turnover of the control-operate flipflop N15 to the operate or O state enables the "true use memory" signal D55 M3 and the "arith. orders" signal D42, P7, 17. The "arith. orders" signal is applied to the grids of "and" circuits P7 and P17. The "true use memory" signal synchronizes the memory and the control for one action cycle, as described in Section 5.13. It should be recalled that the action cycle begins during the action sense pulse with the turnover of the action-regenerate flipflop N17 to the action or 0 state. The action state produces a negative voltage on one grid (pin 5) of "and" circuit P19 and also on one grid (pin 6) of "and" circuit P20. The action sense pulse is followed by the delay pulse which is followed in turn by the up counter pulse. The up counter pulse is applied to the other grid (pin 6) of P19 and the cathode of P19 goes negative. A negative signal is then produced on one grid of each of the four "and" circuits P13, 14, 7, 8. The second grid of "and" circuit P7 has been pulled negative by the "arith orders" signal, so that the cathode of P7 is now negative. The clear voltage is generated in P3a and P2b and is transmitted to the RCR^3 driver driver chassis (Drawing 194) and eventually enables the red clear in R^3. The RCR^3 voltage is applied through "or" circuit M64b, 65 to the plate of the checking flipflop M66, setting it to the 0 state. The length of the red clear is determined by the length of the up counter pulse.

Approximately 12 μ sec after the end of the up counter pulse, the writing dash pulse begins. The action state of N17 and the writing dash pulse enable "and" circuit P20 which, with the "arith orders" signal enables "and" circuit P17. The gate voltage is generated in N11 and is transmitted through the gate driver circuit (Drawing 280) to enable the Green Gate in R^3. The green gate, through "or" circuit M52 and gate circuit M53, sets the checking flipflop M67 to the 0 state. The 0 state

165

of M67 and the 0 state flipflop M66 enable "and" circuit M68, which
then provides the "have cleared and gated" signal to the control.
The duration of the gate signal is approximately that of the writing dash pulse.

The next action sense pulse, which begins approximately
2 μ sec. after the end of the writing dash pulse, returns the
action-regenerate flipflop N17 to the regenerate or 1 state, thereby disabling "and" circuits P19 and P20.

The transfer of order pairs from the memory and the synchronous gating of the R and A orders are similarly executed. Separate
checking circuits (M49a, 50, 51, 61, 62) are provided for the transfer of order pairs from the memory. The order pair transfer checking flipflops M61, are reset to the 1 state by the operate or 0
state of the control-operate flipflop N15. The number transfer
checking flipflops M66,67 are reset to the 1 state by the control
or 1 state of flipflop N15. Resetting voltages are generated by
bleeding up normal flipflop voltages by approximately 10 v. The
resistance networks used for this purpose are located between the
cathode followers of N21 and those of N22 (Drawing 290).

5.16 THE DISPATCH COUNTER. In the design of a digital
computer using a single address code and having a Williams type
memory, it is necessary to include a control counter for sequencing orders and a regeneration counter for controlling regeneration
of successive memory locations. The number of stages of each of the

166

binary counters -- ten in ORDVAC -- is determined by the number
of storage locations in the memory. The counting process in the
regeneration counter occurs during the regeneration cycles; in
the control counter, the counting process occurs during the action
cycles. Since regeneration cycles and action cycles are mutually
exclusive timewise, it is possible to combine certain of the
operations in the counting process. The resultant combination
control and regeneration counter is called the dispatch counter.

The counting process is quite straightforward. The process will be described for the regeneration counter; with slight
changes in terminology, the description applies to the control
counter. At the beginning of the regeneration cycle, the number
under consideration is located in the regeneration register. The
common or dispatch register is cleared by the action sense pulse
and the number in the regeneration register is gated to the dispatch register by the up counter pulse. Circuits consisting
essentially of one-half adder and one carry circuit per digit
generate the next address to be regenerated. The regeneration
register is then cleared by the writing dash pulse and the output
of the half adders is gated by the dash end pulse to the regeneration register to complete the counting process.

The half adder and carry generating circuits and the dispatch register are common to both counters. The inputs to the
half adder circuit of each of the nine most significant stages are
(1) the carry from the previous stage and (2) the corresponding
digit of the dispatch register. For the least significant digit,

167

the half adder inputs are (1) the least significant digit of the dispatch register and (2) a negative voltage indicative of a 1. Under these conditions, the outputs of the half adders represent a 10 digit binary number which is one greater than the number in the dispatch register. The half adder outputs can be gated to either the regeneration register or to the order register.

The address generator senses the dispatch register during all regeneration cycles and during many action cycles as well. It is important that the dispatch register should indicate the desired address during the time the beam is turned on in each of the cathode ray tubes in the memory. In terms of the pulses listed in Section 5.13, the beam is turned on at the beginning of the writing dash pulse and is turned off -- at the very latest -- during the dash end pulse. The address is gated into the dispatch register by the up counter pulse at least 9μsec. before the beam is turned on. The dispatch register is cleared to 0 by the action sense pulse after the beam has been turned off.

Dispatch Counter Circuits. The dispatch counter chassis (Drawing 274) is a 9 row, 12 column chassis. Columns 1 and 2 contain clear driver and gate driver circuits for the three ten-digit registers of the dispatch counter. Columns 3 to 12 contain the registers, gates, and logical circuits of the dispatch counter. The flipflops of row 1 form the regeneration register, those of row 5 form the dispatch register, and those of row 9 form the control register. Rows 2 and 8 (col. 3-12) are gate tubes for the following four gates:

(1) Tubes of columns 3, 5, 7, 9 and 11, row 2 are used to gate from the regeneration register to the dispatch register. This gate is called the B_r gate.

(2) Tubes of columns 3, 5, 7, 9 and 11, row 8 are used to gate from the control register to the dispatch register. (B_0 gate).

(3) Tubes of columns 4, 6, 8, 10, 12 row 2 are used to gate the half adder outputs to the regeneration register. (A_r gate).

(4) Tubes of columns 4, 6, 8, 10 and 12, row 8 are used to gate the half adder outputs to the control register. (A_0 gate).

The remaining tubes in the dispatch counter, namely rows 3, 4, 6 and 7 (columns 3-12) contain the logical circuits which generate the carry and half adder outputs.

The logical diagram of the half adder and carry circuits with gating for one counter is included in Drawing 274. A carry is generated in the nth stage in the "and" circuit of row 3 if a carry was generated in the (n - 1)th stage(the stage to the left) and if the flipflop in the nth stage of the common register is in the 1 state. To prevent deterioration of a carry signal through a number of stages, circuits of the type shown in row 4, column 4 are inserted in each even column of row 4. This carry regeneration circuit is not shown on the logical diagram. The half adder circuit is composed of the inverters of row 7, odd columns; the "and" circuits of rows 3 and 6; and the "or" circuits of row 7, even columns. Grids of the A gate tubes in the nth stage are negative under two conditions:

(1) The flipflop of the nth stage is in the 1 state and a carry is generated in the (n-1)th stage,

(2) The flipflop of the nth stage is in the 0 state and a carry is not generated in the (n-1)th stage.
If the grid of an A gate tube is negative, the flipflop of the order or regeneration register is left in the 0 state to which it has previously been cleared, otherwise the A gate tube draws current and sets the flipflop to the 1 state.

DISPATCH COUNTER GATING. Circuits in the memory control chassis control dispatch counter gating to accomplish the following:

(1) During each regeneration cycle and during each false use memory action cycle, the address in the regeneration counter is increased by 1;

(2) During each action cycle involving the transfer of an order pair from the memory, the address in the order counter is increased by 1;

(3) During each false use memory action cycle, the address in the order register R_3 is gated to the control register.

The clearing and gating necessary for increasing the regeneration address by 1 may be summarized as follows:

(1) The flipflops of the dispatch register are cleared to 0's by the action sense pulse,

(2) The up counter pulse enables the B_r gate which transfers the contents of the regeneration register to the dispatch register,

(3) The flipflops of the regeneration register are cleared to 0's by the writing dash pulse,

(4) The dash end pulse enables the A_r gate which transfers the next higher regeneration address to the regeneration register.

The same process is used for increasing the control address by 1, except that the control register is used and the B_o and A_o gates are enabled.

Transfer of an address from the order register R_3 to the control register of the dispatch counter is also effected by clearing and gating in synchronism with the memory pulses. The flipflops of the control register are first cleared to 0's by the up counter or the writing dash pulse. A checking flipflop is provided to check that the gating has occurred.

Circuit Used for Dispatch Counter Gating. Positive controlling signals are generated in the logical circuits of M22, 34, 59, and 63. Clearing and gating signals are generated in the circuits of M11b, 12, 23, 24, 36, 47, 48, 60, 71a and 72. The circuits of M57a, 69, and 70 are used for checking the gating from R_3 to the control register.

171

The three conditions for synchronous gating in the dispatch counter correspond to enabling signals in the memory control circuitry. The enabling signals which are positive are as follows:

(1) The "regeneration or false use memory" signal which enables counting in the regeneration counter is formed by M34,

(2) The "false use memory and action" signal which enables gating to the dispatch counter from R_3 is formed by M59,

(3) The "control and action" signal which enables counting in the control counter, is formed by M22.

Typical clear-gate sequences are the clear control register, A_o gate sequence and the clear regeneration register, A_r gate sequence. If the former sequence is desired, the "control and action" signal (M22) is positive and the grids of M24a and M48a are positive. When the writing dash pulse pulls the cathode of M24 negative, the order register is cleared by the action of M12a and of the 5687's of row 9, columns 1 and 2 of the dispatch counter. When the dash end pulse occurs, the cathode of M48 is negative and the A_o gate is enabled through M60b and the circuits of row 6, column 1 and row 8, columns 1 and 2 of the dispatch counter. If the "regenerate or false use memory" signal is positive, the grids of M24b and M48b are positive and the writing dash pulse and dash end pulse enable the clear regeneration register, A_r gate sequence.

During true use memory action cycles, none of the three dispatch counter enabling signals listed above is positive. The circuits have been designed in such a way that the control address appears in the common register during true use memory action cycles. (The reasons for this design will be discussed in connection with order pair test procedure, Section 5.19.) The dispatch register is always cleared by the action sense pulse. In all cases an address is gated to the dispatch register during the up counter pulse. If regenerate or false use memory (M34) is positive, the B_r gate is enable through M47b and M36a. If the cathode of M34 is negative, the output of inverter M63 is positive and the B_o gate is enabled through M47a and M60a. The cathode of M34 is negative during control action cycles and during true use memory action cycles as well.

The Delay Pulse. The delay pulse is used to prevent spurious dispatch counter gating. If the period of time during which the action sense pulse and the memory enable signal are both negative is short enough, a small negative pulse will appear at the plate (pin 2) of the action-regenerate flipflop N17. This negative pulse will not be of sufficient magnitude to set the flip-flop N17 to the action state, but it will be large enough to appear at the cathode of M34 and on the grid of M63. The inverter M63 amplifies, inverts and delays the pulse to the extent that the grid (pin 6) of M47a is positive during the beginning of the pulse following the action sense pulse. If this following pulse is the up counter pulse, M47a conducts sufficiently to produce a spurious gating signal in the B_o gate circuits. The introduction of the delay pulse eliminates any possibility of spurious gating of this sort.

5.17   INITIATING SIGNALS FOR ARITHMETIC STOP CHASSIS.
The interplay control supplies two initiating signals to the arithmetic stop chassis, as follows:

(1)   The reset enable, which initiates the resetting of the shift counter to 0;

(2)   The go enable, which enables clearing and gating sequences in the accumulator and arithmetic registers.

It is necessary to supply both of these enabling signals for all orders using clearing and gating sequences in the accumulator and arithmetic registers. These orders are conveniently classified in three groups:

(1)   The arithmetic orders, which include the eight addition orders, the multiplication orders, and the divide order;

(2)   The shift and the input-output orders; namely, the left shift, the right shift, the input and the print orders;

(3)   The eight A orders.
Corresponding to these three groups of orders are three signals manufactured in the decoding chassis, called "arith. (Op)" (D42, M19, 44 P7, 17), "LS v RS v Print v Input (Op)" (D43 M31), and "A(Op)" (D41, M18, 19, 45, P8, 18).

Preliminary steps in the execution of the above groups of orders are automatically programmed in the following manner: The

174

turnover of the control-operate flipflop N15 to the operate 0
state and the turnover of the clear-hold flipflop D65 to the
hold or 0 state after the accumulator has been cleared enable one
of the three order group signals listed above. The reset enable
signal will go negative and the memory enable signal will also
go negative if an action cycle is desired. When the counter has
been reset and when the action cycle, if any, is completed, the
go enable signal will be negative and the execution of those steps
of the order involving use of the arithmetic unit will begin.
Thus, if use of the memory is involved in the execution of the
order, the shift counter will be reset during the memory access
time; otherwise the arithmetic unit phase of the execution will
be delayed until the shift counter has been reset.

Detailed Description of Circuits. Logical circuits used
for generation of initiating signals for the arithmetic stop chassis
are shown on Drawing 348. The signals "A (Op)", (D14 M19), "Arith.
(Op)" (D42 M19), and "LS v RS v Print v Input" (D43 M31) are applied
as inputs to "or" circuit M19, 31a. As a result, the grid of M35b
is negative, which enables "and" circuit M35b B9 which, in turn
enables the resetting of the counter. Completion of the resetting
process enables all inputs to "and" circuit B15, 24a, M71b with
the possible exception of the grid of M71b. For the shift or input-
output orders, the grid of M71b is enabled when the counter resetting process begins. The signal "LS v RS v Print v Input" is
applied to "or" circuit M43, 31b and the grid of M71b is enabled

through the double inverter M58. For the A orders and the arithmetic orders, an action cycle must be completed before the grid of M71b is enabled. During the action cycle of the A orders, the address is transferred from R_3 to the control counter and a number is transferred from R_2 to R^3. During the action cycle of the arithmetic orders, a number is transferred from the memory to R^3. For either group of orders, the number transfer to R^3 enables the "have cleared and gated" signal (M68) and completion of the action cycle enables the "have used memory" signal (N6). These signals in turn enable "and" circuit M56. The transfer of the address in R^3 to the control counter enables the "have gated to dispatch counter" signal (M57a). If all transfers have been properly executed, completion of the action cycle enables "or" circuit M43, 31b through "and" circuit M44 for the arithmetic orders or through "and" circuit M45, 57b for the A orders. In this way the initiating signal is supplied for clearing and gating sequences in the arithmetic unit.

5.18 GENERATION OF COMPLETION SIGNALS AND THE COMPLETION FLIPFLOP. When all steps necessary for the execution of an order have been completed, a completion signal is generated. For the orders of ORDVAC, the following six completion signals are generated:

(1) The (C) signal is enabled in the decoding chassis for conditional control transfer orders if the sign digit of the accumulator register is a 1;

176

(2) The e ($\bar{C}$) signal is enabled after the address has been transferred from R_3 to the control counter during the execution of a control transfer order;

(3) The e (Stop) signal is enabled after the address transfer from R_3 to the control counter has been completed if the conditional stop is to be ignored;

(4) The e (R) signal is enabled after a word has been transferred from the memory to the arithmetic register for execution of the R order;

(5) The e (E) signal is enabled after a word or address has been read into the memory from the accumulator register R_1 for execution of the M, E, or E' order;

(6) The e (Arith. Orders) signal is enabled at the completion of all orders which utilize the arithmetic stop chassis and shift sequencing chassis in their programming. These orders include the eight A orders, the shift orders, the print and input orders, and the addition, multiplication, and division orders.

In cases (2) through (5) listed above, the transfer of a word or of an address is essentially all that is required for the execution of the order. In all of these cases, the clearing and gating necessary for effecting the transfer is executed in synchronism with the memory. The "have used memory" signal is therefore sensed in the generation of the corresponding completion signal.

Any one of the completion signals will set the completion

177

flipflop to the 1 state, which in turn sets the control-operate flipflop to the control state. This indirect means of setting the control-operate flipflop is employed to insure that the "memory enable" signal is interrupted during each operate sequence. The interruption is accomplished in the following manner. Initially, the completion flipflop is set to the 0 state during the control state of the operate-control flipflop. During the operate sequence, the 0 state of the completion flipflop is sensed in the generation of the "memory enable" signal. Thus, when one of the completion signals sets the completion flipflop to the 1 state, the "memory enable" signal is disabled. The "have used memory" signal is then disabled which in turn enables the turnover of the operate-control flipflop.

Generation of e (C) Signal. It is necessary to generate a signal which is negative if a conditional control transfer is not to be executed. The cathode of "or" circuit D19 is enabled if either conditional control transfer order is in the decoding register. The cathode of "and" circuit D20 is negative if the accumulator sign digit is a 1. This signal after being inverted twice in D39 is one input to "and" circuit D26, the other input being the "operate" side of the operate-control flipflop N15. The cathode of "and" circuit D26 provides the e (C) signal for the interplay control circuits.

Generation of Completion Signals for Control Transfer Conditional Stop, R, and Store Orders. All steps necessary to

178

execute any one of the control transfer, conditional stop,
R, or store orders occur during a single action cycle. The "have
used memory" signal is sensed in the generation of the end signals corresponding to these order groups. The clearing and gating
sequences of the R order which effect transfers from the memory
are checked; proper execution of the sequence enables M68. Similarly, the gating to the dispatch counter of the control transfer
or Stop orders is checked to enable M57a. Each of these checking
signals is combined with the "have used memory" signal in "and"
circuits M56 and M33, respectively. Each completion signal is
formed by combining the signals enabled by the order group with the
"have used memory" signal directly for the store orders, or with
the output of M56 or M33. The completion signals are generated
in M28, M42, M55 and M32.

Generation of Completion Signals for Orders which Utilize
the Arithmetic Stop Chassis. During the last pair of clear-gate
sequences occurring in the execution of orders utilizing the shift
sequencing and arithmetic stop chassis, a signal is generated to
set the stop flipflop B1 to the 0 state. The final black gate or
red gate will then set the end flipflop B6 to the 1 state. When
the black gate signal again goes positive the cathode of "and" circuit B3 is enabled. The B3 cathode signal, called "B end enable"
would serve as a completion signal for all orders utilizing arithmetic stop chassis, except for two conditions:

(1) In multiplication, it is necessary to make a correction if the multiplier is negative;

(2) In the execution of the input order, it is necessary to gate the four binary digits of the tenth sexadecimal character to the accumulator after the cathode of B3 is enabled. A "tape end" signal, which remains positive until the gating is complete, is available in the input circuitry.

The completion signal for all orders utilizing the arithmetic stop chassis is generated by "and" circuit M9, 3a which has as inputs the three signals "B end enable" (B3), the "tape end" signal, and a signal from the 1 side of the multiplication correction flipflop C62 which indicates that no correction is necessary. If a correction is desired, the multiplication correction flipflop C62 will be in the 0 state and the cathode of C64a will be negative. The output of C64a and the "B end enable" signal are inputs to "and" circuit M8. When "and" circuit M8 is enabled, the false control flipflop B4 is set to the 1 state, the reset and stop flipflops B14 and B1 are reset, the false control flipflop B4 is returned to the 0 state, and the correction (a subtraction) begins.

The Completion Flipflop. It is assumed that the execution of an order involving use of the memory has just begun. The completion flipflop N16 is in the 0 state, so that the "Op mem. enable" signal (M10 N28) enables "and" circuit N28 and through "or" circuit N35 requests an action cycle. At the end of the action cycle the "Op mem. enable" and the "have used memory" signals are negative.

The enabling of "or" circuit P22, 23, 24 by one of the completion signals sets the completion flipflop N16 to the 1 state through gate N10b. The "and" circuit of N28 is disabled and the grid of gate N12a goes positive, thereby setting the synchronization flipflop N18 to the 0 state. The "have used memory" signal is disabled and the output of inverter N24b is negative. The cathode of "and" circuit N23 then goes negative, enabling the turnover of the operate-control flipflop to the 1 or control state, and signalling the completion of the instruction. The control state disables the "Op. mem. enable" signal and the completion flipflop is reset to the 0 state by gate N10a. For orders which do not require use of the memory, the "have used memory" signal will be positive and the output of inverter N24b will be negative throughout the execution of the order. "And" circuit N23 will in this case be enabled as soon as the completion flipflop N16 is set to the 1 state by a completion signal.

181

CHAPTER 6

ORDVAC ENGINEERING MAINTENANCE

EVERY HOUR:

    1. Check the filament voltages to insure that each is 6.2 volts excepting the minus 100 circuit which should be set to 5.7 volts.

EVERY EIGHT HOURS:

    1. Check the d.c. voltages on the end panel of the machine.

    2. Check the memory adjustments by running a flaw test; a read-around test.

    3. Run the leapfrog test for twenty minutes.

EVERY TWENTY-FOUR HOURS:

    1. The memory should be checked using an oscilloscope to observe the video signals at each memory chassis while the memory is reversing using the order pair: clear subtract - store.

    2. Check the cooling system to see that the exhaust air from the machine is less than 40 degrees centigrade.

EVERY WEEK:

    1. Check the outputs of the adder and digit resolver circuits for all states of the input digits. If any circuit of the adder deviates by more than 10 volts from its circuit diagram value then that section of the adder should be examined to ascertain why this is so. Similarly, the digit resolver should be checked at the grids of the tubes in Rows 2, 4 and 6 to see that the d.c. voltages are within 20

volts of the circuit diagram values and the output of the digit
resolver should be checked.

2. Run the leapfrog test for 4 hours.

3. Set four main d.c. voltages with a 1/2 of one percent
meter to their correct values to 1/2 of one percent as read on meter.

EVERY MONTH:

1. The grid voltages of the flipflops in R_I R_{II} and R_{III}
should be checked for the negative state to see that the grid voltage
is more than 25 volts negative when the filament voltage for the
ground circuit of the register side is 6 volts or less.

2. The d.c. values of the clear voltages and the gate voltages
should be measured in each register at both the positive values and
the negative values. When the negative states of the gates are checked
it should be done with the filament voltage at 6.4 volts with a large
gate load and a check should be made at 6 volts with a small gate load.
Similarly, a check should be made when the gates are positive and the
filament voltage is 6.0 to see that the multiplier A chassis would
not "hang up".

3. Check the memory pulses to be sure that each is going
from +10 to -10 volts and to see that they are of the proper time
length.

4. While exercising some caution hammer-test the registers,
adder, digit resolver, and the address generator. Very light taps
will be sufficient to show up some tube errors which might cause

183

trouble during the coming month, but it is not necessary to
vigorously hammer-test the circuits.

5. Change the air filters.

EVERY THREE MONTHS:

1. Inspect all power supplies and tubes to see if there
is any appreciable accumulation of dirt and to see that all tubes
are operating (one rectifier could be out without its being known).

EVERY YEAR:

1. Remove the covers from the machine and inspect all
wiring for dirt and dust. If this has accumulated then it should
be removed with a brush and a vacuum cleaner.

AT THE END OF THREE YEARS AND EVERY YEAR THEREAFTER:

Remove all of the electrolytic condensers from the four
main power supplies and check the capacity and leakage of each.
Replace any condensers in which the leakage is excessive or in which
the capacity is low.

CHAPTER 7

OPERATING PROCEDURE

In this chapter a description is presented which will enable the machine to be placed into operation. This requires that the necessary power switches be turned on, that a basic operating test be made, and that the initial input order be placed into the machine. The effects of the various positions of the "operating" switches are also discussed.

7.1 <u>TURNING ON THE MACHINE.</u> Because of the interlocks provided, it is necessary to follow a certain sequence of steps to turn on the machine. These steps are as follows:

1. TURN ON THE BLOWERS. If this is not done an interlock will prevent the application of more than one-half the normal filament voltage on all of the tubes.

2. TURN ON THE MAIN FILAMENT SWITCH. This switch has a time delay relay so that when the switch is first turned on the filament voltage is very low. After about 1 1/2 minutes the delay relay closes and full voltage is applied to the filaments.

3. INSPECT ALL FILAMENT VOLTMETERS. These meters are located on the end of the machine nearest the memory slave tube. The voltages should with one exeeption be set to 6.2 volts. The single

exception is the circuit on the adder side which is pegged at +100 volts. It has been common practice to set this to 5.5 volts.

4. INSPECT THE D-C LINE VOLTMETERS. These meters are located on the end of the machine farthest from the memory slave tube. Inspect meter on memory high voltage power supply.

5. TURN ON THE D-C POWER. This is done by turning to ON the d-c power switch and then pushing the d-c push button. Both of these are located on the switch panel at the end of the registers near the d-c meters.

6. INSPECT MEMORY SLAVE TUBE AND NOTE WHETHER SOME NEONS ARE GLOWING. If everything is normal, a raster should be seen on the slave tube and some neons should be glowing. There may be none on in the registers, but certain control neons should be on. If the d-c power will not stay on it is an indication of a fault. The d-c is fused with a large number of separate circuits, and if any of these fails a holding relay will drop out and shut off the d-c power. Therefore the d-c fuses located inside the door beneath the d-c meters should be checked. Another possibility is the failure of an a-c filament circuit or (rarely) one of the filament voltage checking tubes.

7. INSPECT THE D-C POTENTIALS OF THE FILAMENT CIRCUITS. Many of these are different from ground. The voltage at which each filament circuit is pegged is marked on the meter associated with it, and if the pegging voltage is not at ground potential the neon above the meter should glow. All of the glowing neons should have about the same brightness. The top electrode should glow for

186

the positive voltages and the bottom one should glow for the negative voltage. If any potential is wrong, the trouble should be sought and fixed.

8. TURN ON THE TELETYPE SWITCHES. The Teletype equipment receives some of its power through switches on the Teletype tables. Turn on the two switches beneath the surface at the left of the Teletype input table and turn on the motors of the Teletype units. The motor switch is at the right side near the keyboard of the page printer.

7.2 **BASIC OPERATING TEST.** If all of the steps of Section 7.1 have been carried out and if everything is working properly, it is usually necessary for the machine to be allowed to warm up for about 30 minutes if it has been turned off for any appreciable time. This is to obtain satisfactory memory storage without readjustments. During this waiting period a reversing routine can be run.

The reversing routine is set up by using the switches and push buttons on the operating panel beneath the slave tube. The procedure is as follows:

1. Set the white switch to OPERATE,

2. Set the black switch to RUN,

3. Set the red switch to ORDER PAIRS,

4. Put the "clear accumulator and subtract" order L1000 into the even (left) location of R_3,

5. Put the "store" order 40000 into the odd (right) location of R_3,

6. Throw the white switch to RUN.

The machine should now successively execute the two orders at each memory location in turn. This will repetitively change dots to dashes and dashes to dots. The neons in R_1, R_2 and R^3 will go on and off like a flashing sign.

At the end of its warmup time the memory should be cleared by pressing the MEMORY CLEAR button on the operating panel. It is then easy to see whether or not each of the 39 memory tubes is reversing properly by examing them all with the slave tube and the 40-position switch. Tube 39 does not reverse in this test.

If some memory tube does not reverse properly there is a fault in a register, in the adder - digit resolver, or in the memory. If only a few addresses on some memory tube fail to reverse properly, this is a clear indication that the trouble is associated with that particular memory tube. This will ordinarily be correctable by making relatively minor adjustments of the intensity, focus, or astigmatism controls for the tube in question.

If it is necessary to make this adjustment it is ordinarily necessary to connect up an oscilloscope to observe the video signals coming from the particular memory chassis which shows the trouble. The oscilloscope can easily be synchronized by the use of the dash-end pulse which has been connected to a convenient terminal near the memory rack. The technique of adjusting the memory should normally be carried out while it is attempting to make the clear subtract and store order operate satisfactorily. If the oscilloscope is properly synchronized a very clear indication should be seen for the

188

dashes and dots. An attempt should be made to adjust the three controls so that the oscilloscope traces of the signals from the dots are well grouped, those from the dashes are well grouped, and so that those from the dots do not have a tendency to go positive. For a more detailed discussion of memory adjustment see Section 4.4.

.7.3 PUTTING A PROBLEM INTO ORDVAC. If the requirement of Section 7.1 and 7.2 have been met, it will be possible to put a problem into the machine. There are two ways in which this can be done:

(a) Using order pairs,
(b) Using an input routine.

Order Pairs Method. This method requires the attention of the operator for stopping at the correct place. It is as follows:

1. Set the red switch to ORDER PAIRS,

2. Set the black switch to RUN,

3. Set the white switch to CONTROL with the neon beneath it OFF,

4. Set the control counter to the address at which the first tape word will be stored. If this address is 0, it can be set by pushing the unmarked button on the control panel.

5. Put the order pair 80028 40028 into R_3,

6. Put the tape into the tape reader at the first word to be read,

7. Throw the white switch to RUN,

8. As the last word is being read from the tape, throw the white switch to OPERATE,

9. Move the white switch to CONTROL and back to OPERATE. This will store the last word read in from the tape,

189

10. Set the red switch to NORMAL,

11. Set the control counter to the address of the first word of the program,

12. Throw the white switch to RUN.

The foregoing procedure will put the tape contents into successive memory locations beginning with the address set into the control counter and will then start the program.

Input Routine Method. This method is more elegant and leaves less opportunity for operator error. It requires an input routine, of which there are many kinds. This input routine precedes the main routine on the tape and once it is started assumes complete control of the input operation, requiring no operator attention. It is assumed here that an input routine beginning at address 0 is used.

1. Set the red switch to NORMAL,

2. Set the black switch to RUN,

3. Set the white switch to CONTROL with the neon beneath it OFF,

4. Set the control counter to 0 by pushing the unmarked panel button,

5. Put the order pair 80028 40000 into R_3,

6. Put the tape into the tape reader at the first word to be read,

7. Throw the white switch to RUN.

This is all that is necessary to put in a program and run it. However, the programmer may have coded check stops into the

routine and if this is so the operator will have to move the
black switch to START each time a check stop occurs.

7.4 THE OPERATING PANEL. This panel, located near the
memory slave tube, has 3 switches, 2 pushbuttons and a neon. The
functions of these switches and buttons are as follows:

White Switch. This switch has 3 positions.

1. CONTROL. The result of going to this position
depends upon what has previously taken place. If a right hand
order was just executed, a new order pair will be brought into
R_3 from the memory and one of the orders will be gated to the
decoding register. It will be the left hand order unless the
right hand order executed was an order transferring control to
the right-hand side.

If a left-hand order (not a control transfer order) was
just executed, the right hand order will be gated to the decoding
register. If the left hand order was a control transfer order, a
new order pair will be brought into R_3 from the memory and one of
the orders will be gated to the decoding register.

2. OPERATE. The machine will execute the order gated
to the decoding register when the switch was on CONTROL.

3. RUN. The machine will automatically carry out the
operations which would be performed singly if the switch were moved
back and forth between the CONTROL and OPERATE positions. The RUN
position is the normal operating position.

BLACK SWITCH. This switch has 3 positions:

1. RUN. This is the normal position. When the
switch is in this position the machine will stop whenever it is
presented with the conditional stop order 30.

2. START. If a conditional stop order has been encountered, the machine will start again if the switch is thrown
to START and released. The switch will not stay in the START position.

3. STOP DISABLE. When the switch is in this position
the machine will ignore all conditional stop orders.

RED SWITCH. This switch has two positions.

1. ORDER PAIRS. The machine will indefinitely execute
the order pair in R_3, doing the left and right-hand orders alternately. Moreover, all addresses that normally come from R_3 to the
address generator will now come from the control counter. Other
addresses will be unaffected.

2. NORMAL. This is the usual position of this
switch.

NEON LIGHT. This light is on the A flipflop (Chapter 5,
Part II). When the white switch is on CONTROL and the neon is OFF,
the machine will execute the left hand order next.

MEMORY CLEAR BUTTON. When pushed this button will clear the
memory to dots (1's) in every location

UNMARKED BUTTON. When pushed this button will set the
control counter to zero.

During the normal running of a program, the effect will be

192

disastrous if either pushbutton or the red switch is used. No harm will result from moving the white or black switches.

CHAPTER 8

TROUBLE SHOOTING TECHNIQUES

There is no magic formula or apparatus which will provide the answer to every maintenance problem. An efficient trouble-shooter must be intimately familiar with the logical structure of the machine, and such familiarity will in general come only with experience. A few words of advice seem desirable in this matter, however.

The machine is a complex arrangement of elementary circuits. Fixing any individual circuit will usually be a simple matter for a person with a basic understanding of vacuum tube circuits. Locating the particular elementary circuit at fault among the hundreds of faultless circuits, however, poses a problem of major proportions. Quite obviously the total number of failures that could occur in a machine having 2700 vacuum tubes is immense. Assuming that only tubes could be at fault one sees that the task of compiling a table of symptoms and causes would be a prohibitively long one. As a result, the only way to find a faulty circuit is to follow some sort of logical procedure which is calculated to find the most difficult error in the shortest time. Short cuts can always be found which will take care of special cases with a saving in time and effort. In general, these will be learned by experience.

The computer can be divided into four primary subparts: They are the input-output, the arithmetic unit, the control and the memory. If possible the first step in the resolution of any failure should be to isolate the error by reasoning, test, or measurements to one of these primary subparts.

8.1 FINDING THE FAULT. Quite often the major problem is deciding in which of the main subparts the trouble lies. The procedure for doing this cannot very well be dictated since the particular type of failure will determine the exact procedure to be used. The most difficult type of failure to resolve is one which causes the machine to make an error but which allows the program to proceed through the problem as though everything were correct. In such a case the only clue to the failure is that the answer is different from the predicted one or from the previously calculated one. To find such an error it is essential that some-one who knows the details of the program be available for trouble-shooting.

Printing Out the Memory. The first step is usually to examine the contents of the memory. This may be done simply by printing out (by order-pairs) the entire contents of the memory or by running a comparison routine whereby only those memory words are printed out which disagree with the corresponding words on the problem tape. Input, Subtract, Conditional Transfer, Store and Print orders are used in this routine and must be working. From a machine standpoint, the order pairs technique is safer since

195

it employs only the R and Print orders. The printed results must then be compared with a written copy of the routine, however, which admits the element of human error. It is obviously important to know which memory locations are used for variable storage and which orders may be changed by the routine itself in order to be able to interpret the results properly.

Analysis of the Print-Out. From the nature of the discrepancy (if any) between memory contents and tape, it may be possible to deduce where the trouble lies.

a. Memory Indications. If several orders are missing zeros in a particular binary digit, then very probably one digit of the memory is not storing dashes properly. Looking at the memory amplifier signals should enable one to confirm this diagnosis, however, before corrective measures are applied. If too many zeros appear in one digit, there may be random errors appearing in one memory tube. A short waiting period while the memory stores only dots may show that particular tube to be picking up random dashes. Tapping the suspected memory chassis lightly may help also.

b. Adder-Digit Resolver Indication. If the orders which appear to be incorrect in the memory are used as counting indices, etc., and are passed through the adder, then the adder or digit resolver may be suspected. Numerical contents may indicate an adder failure also. Here one should use a test routine which tells whether the adder is functioning properly in every state of every digit, and whether the computer is capable of properly executing all the other orders. An alternative procedure is to proceed stepwise through the problem which has failed by manipulating the Operate-Control switch and observing the treatment of the numbers in the registers. This alternative procedure is only practical, however, in the case of short routines or short parts of long routines. It should be emphasized that once the trouble has been isolated to a particular part of the machine the complicated routine should be set aside and a short, simple routine written which will rapidly and continuously test that suspected part or order.

d. Control Indications. It may sometimes happen that the routine will not proceed to the end and give an answer. In such a case the machine may simply hang up and refuse to proceed past one particular state of the control. This state is defined as the combined status of the individual control flipflops. There are several ways in which this can happen. The control safety circuits which check to see that the clears and gates have been performed' properly may fail. The clears and gates themselves may fail. An order may have been brought out of the memory improperly, such that the control does not recognize the order. Or one of the completion signals may fail to appear at the end of an order execution.

c. Input-Output Indication. If the numbers stored in the memory are incorrect, and have been printed out for inspection,

the difficulty may lie with the input equipment. If the problem is read into the memory and read out again immediately before
any part of the problem is done, the only errors possible are input
errors, writing errors and random errors in the memory. A reversing pattern order pair (clear-subtract and store) should prove
whether or not the memory is capable of large-scale writing failures.
If the memory reverses properly for several minutes the blame can
probably be laid on the input. Input test routines exist which read
a number from a continuous tape and compare it with a number stored
in the memory.

    8.2 <u>MALFUNCTIONS IN THE ARITHMETIC UNIT.</u> In the event that
the trouble appears to be in the arithmetic unit (a sum or a shift
is incorrect), there are four switches on the control panel farthest
from the slave tube which allow the addition or shift to be halted
after individual clears or gates so that the results of each operation can be examined. Table 8.1 gives the switches, called clear and
gate stop switches:

RC/BC   GG/YG   YC/GC   BG/RG

Table 8.1

Clear and Gate Stop Switches

When RC/BC is thrown to STOP, the operation of the machine will be
suspended with the red or black clear on. If the GG/YG switch is
put to STOP and the RC/BC switch is returned to normal, the red

(or black) clear will go off and the green (or yellow) gate will
go down and remain down as long as the switch is kept on STOP.
To proceed to the next step, the YC/GC switch is thrown to STOP
and the GG/YG switch is then returned to normal. Then the green
(or yellow) gate will go off and allow the yellow (or green) clear
to come on and stay on. The negative voltages of the clears and
gates can be measured with a d-c voltmeter by proper use of these
switches.

Once isolated to a main subpart, the error can be found
by redividing the main subpart at some convenient place in its
logical structure and deciding in which half the error then appears.
By such continued binary divisions the trouble can be most efficiently
localized.

After the particular circuit at fault has been located, its
specific trouble can be diagnosed by using a voltmeter or an oscilloscope to observe what is happening. When measurements are made
with a voltmeter, it is not often necessary to calculate the loading
effect of the meter. However, attention must be given to the output
impedance of the circuit being measured, and if the impedance is
high enough a correction must be made on the voltmeter reading.

8.3 MALFUNCTIONS IN THE CONTROL. If one of the clears
(or gates) or the safety circuits associated with them have failed,
the machine will not proceed. Toggles T_c and T_g in the shift sequencing chassis may hold the answer immediately. Table 8.2 shows
the states of T_c and T_g which exist during each of the clears and
gates.

199

T_c	T_g	OPERATION
1	1	RC or BC
0	1	GG or YG
0	0	GC or YC
1	0	RG or BG

Table 8.2

Clear and Gate Enabling Signals

If the program is arrested with T_c and T_g in any except the 1-1 state, it should be very easy to find the circuit which is causing the trouble. Assume, for example, that the yellow clear is being held on in R_1. The fact that it is on can be determined by a d-c measurement, or by simply noting that it is impossible to turn on any of the flipflops in R_1. The trouble may be in the cathode follower chain between R_1 and R_2,which would cause YCR_2 to be off. Since it is YCR_2 which turns T_c on, the T_c-T_g state would be 0-0.

If YCR_1 and YCR_2 are both on and T_c is off, then the trouble must lie between YCR_2 and T_c, or with T_c itself. Measurements with a d-c voltmeter along the chain of circuits between the two should show up any trouble which might be present.

If YCR_1 and YCR_2 are both down, but T_c is equal to 1, then there is some difficulty within the clear forming circuit or the clear drivers which is holding the clears down, since $T_c = 1$ ($T_g = 0$) is the signal for the black gate. The black gate cannot turn on until the YCR_2 has turned off. Here again d-c measurements

200

along the chain from the output of T_c and T_g to the clear drivers
should show up the trouble. Ramifications of these problems and
solutions should be apparent. The fact that the clear (or gate)
is or is not on, and the state of the flipflops in the shift sequencing chassis should be sufficient knowledge to allow isolation
of the trouble to a particular chain of circuits. In the event
that T_c and T_g are both on there are several things which might
cause trouble. If the red (or black) clear in R^1 (and/or R^2)
is down, then the above remarks apply. If, however, the clear is not
on, there is no information from the shift sequencing chassis to
indicate what the trouble may be. If the STOP flipflop in the arithmetic stop chassis is on, then the machine has been stopped by the
shift sequencing chassis, in the clear forming circuits, or by some
of the other signals coming to the shift sequencing chassis which
enable the first clear. There are many signals which come into
this chassis and which could inhibit the first clear. The "0" and
"1" signals, for example, come from all parts of the control. One
of them must be negative for the clear. If one is not negative, then
the trouble lies in that group of inputs. There are other enabling
signals which must also be present. They come from the delay selector chassis, the arithmetic stop chassis, the arithmetic control,
and the memory control. If the shift sequencing chassis is being held
up by the absence of one of these external signals, it will be
necessary to make d-c measurements within the several control chassis

involved until the trouble is isolated.

Synchronous Control Failure. There are other troubles
which can show up in the control, but for those asynchronous parts
where the first operation must be ended before another can begin,
the same sort of d-c technique just described can be profitably
applied.

In the case of some of the memory control circuits which
are driven from the pulser, and hence are necessarily synchronous,
the d-c technique is not directly applicable. Generally it is
easier to use an oscilloscope to diagnose the problem. The circuits
in the pulsers, clock, dispatch counter, and memory synchronization
chassis are notable examples of this type of circuit. However, if
it develops that the circuit is completely inoperative, and the
trouble is difficult to find with an oscilloscope, a battery and
switch can sometimes be substituted for the pulse in question, and
the d-c technique resorted to. When the fault appears in a synchronous
part of the machine, and the oscilloscope is used, there are several
precautions that must be observed. If the input to the oscilloscope
represents a large capacitance in the circuit, it is quite possible
that hanging the oscilloscope lead on the circuit will change the
circuit in such a way that it will fail, even though it is not normally faulty. On the other hand, the oscilloscope capacitance may
also cause a failing circuit to behave quite normally as long as it
is being observed. If the output impedance of the circuit in question
is high, this loading problem can be helped somewhat by using a

202

cathode follower to feed into the oscilloscope.

When the waveforms on the oscilloscope are observed, a greater amount of information can be obtained if both deflection and intensity modulations are used than if only the normal deflection modulation is observed. For example, if it is desired to see the output of the adder or digit resolver during a particular sequence of orders, then it should be possible to find an order which is performed only once - - like a transfer of control - - during the routine which is suspected. By synchronizing the sweep with this signal the pulses will be caused to appear on the oscilloscope in the order in which they are normally created by the routine. By causing the oscilloscope trace to bright up on a particular order (or gate) the part of the trace which is of primary interest will stand out and that part which is of lesser interest will be suppressed. The bright parts of the trace will then represent those orders (or gates) in the proper order commencing with the first one executed after the order on which the sweep is initiated.

An additional oscilloscope aid in matters of this sort would be a recognition circuit which would uniquely recognize one and only one state of the order or regeneration counter. This signal could be used for the scope trigger, so that the sweep would be initiated whenever a particular count had been reached. This would be of interest, for example, whenever it would be desired to observe the memory signals at one particular address in the memory during a problem or read-around test. Thirty-five tubes is a fair estimate of the requirements of such a circuit.

8.4 MALFUNCTIONS IN THE MEMORY. When it has been decided that the program failed because of a memory error, it will generally also be known which digit is at fault and whether the change was from a 0 to a 1, a 1 to a 0, or both.

Flaws. If the memory position changed a 0 to a 1 at one address only, the trouble may be a flaw on the face of the tube at that address. This can be verified by running a flaw finding routine. If the flaw does exist, there are generally three possible procedures. (1) The signals should be examined for low intensity and bad focus, and the tube readjusted to compensate for any changes in these adjustments. (2) If that does not work, the raster can be moved slowly while a flaw-finding routine is running until no address in any of the forty tubes is situated on a flaw. (3) This also may not be possible, and the third possibility is to exchange the faulty cathode ray tube for a spare which is believed more nearly free of flaws.

Low Intensity. If the memory position shows more than one address with dots where dashes had been stored, it is probable that the intensity has drifted down to a low condition, or that the amplifier gain has fallen off. It should be easy to tell from the amplifier signals which case is true.

Random Dashes and Read-around Troubles. If the contents
of one memory position has too many zeros (dashes) it is possible
that the position has made random errors of the most common type
or that the read-around ratio of that tube is lower than the ratio
required by the code being performed. To confirm that the position
is picking up random dashes it should only be necessary to allow
the memory to sit quietly for a few minutes with a raster of all
dots. Any errors which do occur will be perpetuated. If the
position does make errors, the most likely suspect is the chassis.
It may show a tendency to pick up extra dashes when it is tapped
slightly. Even if it does not it may still be at fault, and if no
other cause for the trouble can definitely be found, then the chassis
should be replaced with a good one. Of course, the trouble may lie
with the 3KP1. Most 3KP1's will cause changes in their signals when
they are tapped, even lightly, so care must be taken not to be too
hasty about blaming the cathode ray tube.

Miscellaneous Memory Malfunctions. There should be very little
trouble with anything associated with the rack position itself.
The focus and intensity controls are well insulated from ground, and
the bypass capacitors for each stage are also fairly well insulated.
The grid coupling capacitor may give some trouble. If a piece of
solder or wire or dirt should intermittently short one of the capacitor cases to ground, or if the high voltage wire should develop
small arcs, the symptoms will appear as dashes in identical addresses

on many of the tubes. If the output of any one of the amplifiers is observed while the intensity of its 3KP1 is turned completely off, a signal unique to a high voltage arc will be seen. The amplifier output will be quite large in both directions, sufficient to saturate the amplifier. Such an arc can be found most easily by successively dividing the high voltage circuit into halves until the stage or wire at fault is isolated. When this division process is performed, it is important that the slave tube and its high voltage circuits not be forgotten. Occasionally a clue can be obtained by listening carefully, since a severe arc can be heard and some can even be seen.

If there have been failures in the same address on more than one 3KP1, and if the amplifier signal associated with a high voltage arc is not found, then the address generator, counter, pulser, or other components associated with all forty memory positions in parallel should be suspected.

The following outline gives a standard procedure for testing the memory chassis.

8.5 CHASSIS TEST PROCEDURE.

I. D-C Leakage Test, Connect +300v from +300v bus to ground with 20,000 Ω/v voltmeter in series with + lead.

    A. Chassis passes if:

        1. Tapping on V14, 15, 16, 1, 2, 3, 4 causes less than 2μa fluctuation of leakage current.

        2. Total leakage current is less than 5μa and is not due to one tube.

3. Tapping on ceramic feed through, mica by-pass, and bathtube condensers causes no fluctuation of leakage current.

B. Replace any components which do not pass above tests.

II. Standard preventive repairs and changes.

A. Check and resolder any suspicious ground connections in amplifier section.

B. Wire V1 socket for 6AU6 (Connect pins 2 and 7).

C. Solder ground lug to screw head in approximate center of logical section and put lock washer under nut on the screw of this same terminal.

III. Insert chassis in WIIA and adjust CRT for satisfactory static storage if possible.

A. Check for amplifier microphonics.

1. Tap chassis near plug end while observing amplifier output; if trace jumps 1/4 dash height, chassis is not acceptable. (Use judgment on severity of tapping).

2. Ground successive 6AK5 grids to isolate stage at fault. Replace faulty 6AK5 if any of last three stages is at fault and replace V1 with 6AU6 if first stage is at fault.

A. Check for other intermittent troubles.

1. Tap all other tubes and circuit wiring (with care) and watch slave tube for any suspicious intermittent phenomenon. Be particularly sure of last few stages of chassis (V14, 15, 16) and first few stages of logical circuit (V5, 6, 7).

207

C. Check chassis for all functions.

    1. Check reversing.

    2. Check one shot write in, (dots and dashes).

D. Special procedures for particular complaints.

    1. Check amplifier gain if complaint is:

        a. Low gain,

        b. Insufficient output (Check V4),

        c. Other complaints which might indicate low gain,

        d. Also check gain if intensity must be set too high to allow reversing in order to store statically. Gain of over 40,000 should be maintained when measured with a 1.3 µs pulse of $25 \times 2.87 \times 10^{-5}$ v. (Dash test pulse sent through attenuator) Output should be greater than 28v peak.

    2. Check logical circuits if complaint is:

        a. Won't write dots (dashes),

        b. Beam on all the time,

        c. Won't store dots (dashes).

    3. Test storage and signals from amplifier with 5% transient drop and 5% ripple on each of the four DC supplies.

E. Static storage test. Run chassis in WIIA on static storage of a pattern for as long as practical or until obvious failure.

CHAPTER 9

POWER CIRCUITS

9.1 <u>GENERAL DISTRIBUTION</u>. The ORDVAC requires primary
power to operate its filaments and the power supplies which
supply the direct current voltages. This primary power (60
cycles per second) is distributed as follows:

USE	POTENTIAL (VOLTS)	CURRENT (AMPERES)
-300v, +100v, +150v, +300v power supplies	208, 220 or 230 three phase	50
+680v power supply	115 single phase	10
-2000v power supply	115 single phase	15
Memory filament circuit (through a regulating transformer)	115 single phase	22
Register side filament circuits	115 single phase	40
Adder side filament circuits	115 single phase	40
Input-Output equipment	115 single phase	10

9.2 <u>MAIN DIRECT CURRENT SUPPLIES</u>. The power supplies
supplying -300v, +100v, +150v and +300v have the type numbers
615D, 615B, 615B and 615A respectively. They were manufactured

by the Power Equipment Company, 55 Antoinette Street, Detroit 2, Michigan. These power supplies have current ratings as follows:

-300 volts, 25 amperes (but 20 amperes for pulse and.
                    ripple specifications which follow)

+100 volts, 25 amperes

+150 volts, 25 amperes

+300 volts, 15 ameres

The +100 volt and +150 volt power supplies are identical and interchangeable if several taps are changed. The voltage standards for all power supplies are VR type gas tubes. The power supplies are designed for continuous operation with an external ambient temperature of 100° F.

The output electrolytic capacitors (about .05 farads for the 100-150 volt supplies and about .02 farads for the 300 volt supplies) together with the regulating circuit provided were designed to meet the following regulation specification:

The DC output voltage will be held constant within $\pm$ 2% on an instantaneous basis as observed on an oscilloscope due to any combination or all of the following:

(a) Line voltage change of $\pm$ 10% from nominal tap setting,

(b) Keyed load changes from.zero to full load which take place at in any length of time not less than one microsecond.

(c) Ripple because of inadequate "filtering".

Drawings for these power supplies (as well as spare parts) are furnished but not in this manual.

9.3 SMALL POWER SUPPLIES. Two small power supplies are used: a -2000 volt supply for the memory which has a load of about .075 ampere and a +680 volt supply for the digit resolver which has a load of about .4 ampere. These power supplies are described in drawings M169 and M126 respectively.

9.4 D.C. TURN-ON. In order to turn on the d.c. for the machine it is necessary that filament power be on. In order for the d.c. to stay on after the push button is released it is necessary that all the d.c. voltages be on (i.e. no fuses blown), and that no filament voltages be off. The interlocking relay and tube circuit to check that these conditions have been met is shown in drawing M-129. Drawing S-297 shows the wiring of the "three step" d.c. turn on. The d.c. is turned on in this way to limit the surge currents which charge the condensers and thus reduce the interference to the d.c. power lines in case they are used for other purposes.

9.5 FILAMENT CIRCUITS. The filament circuits are shown on drawing M-190. "Booster" transformers are used in some cases to enable the operator to adjust the filament voltage of circuits carrying large amounts of power with a small five ampere Variac. The filament transformers are located in the base of the machine and are on either the "register side" or. the "adder side". The loads associated with each of these circuits are given in Table 9.1.

I <u>Register Side</u>   TRANSFORMERS BOOSTERS FUSE

    A. Ground Peg

1. Registers	302.4 Amps			
2. Green Gates	25.2			
3. Order Gates	21.9			
4. End. Conn.	8.4			
5. Comp. Gates	32.4			
6. Gate Drivers	10.8			
7. Comp. Gate Drivers	1.8			
8. Driver II	1.2			
9. Address Gen.	25.2			
Total	429.3 Amps	43	3	30

    B. +65V Peg

1. Comp. Gate Driver	5.4 Amps	1	Variac	3

    C. +100V Peg

1. Driver III	1.8 Amp			
2. Clear Drivers	59.4			
3. Clear Driver II	16.2			
4. Address Gen.	10.4			
Total	87.8 Amps	9	1	10

    D. -2000V Peg

1. C.R.T. and diodes	36.9 Amp	4	Sola	20

II. <u>Adder Side</u>

    A. Ground Peg

1. Memory Control	28.5 Amp
2. Dispatch Counter	46.8
3. Pulser C.F.	32.4
4. Adder	24.0
5. Carry Delay	3.8
6. Delay Selector	4.7
7. Multiplier "A"	13.8

Table 9.1
6.3 Volt Filament Loads

212

			TRANSFORMERS	BOOSTERS	FUSE
8.	Multiplier "B"	8.0			
9.	Shift Counter	21.6			
10.	Counter Output	1.8			
11.	Arithmetic Control	28.4			
12.	Decoding Chassis	26.9			
13.	In/out S. and S.	1.7			
14.	TPR Output	0.6			
15.	Memory Sync.	14.1			
16.	Register Selection	8.25			
	Total	265.35	26	2	20

B. +50V Peg

1.	Memory Chassis	202 Amp			
2.	Pulser	20 Amp			
	Total	222 Amp	22#	Sola	20

C. +100V Peg

1.	Multiplier "A"	2.7 Amp			
2.	Multiplier "B"	3.6			
3.	Dispatch Counter	4.5			
4.	Slave C.F.	6			
5.	Register Selection	1.8			
6.	Memory Control	3.6			
	Total	22.2	2	Variac	3

D. +150V Peg

1.	Adder	63.6 Amp			
2.	Digit Resolver	36			
3.	Pulser	3.9			
	Total	103.5 Amp	12	1	8

E. +240V Peg

1.	6AS7 C.F.	30 Amp	3	Variac	3

#: Five of these 22 transformers are on the "adder side".

Table 9.1 Continued
6.3 Volt Filament Loads

Continued   <u>TRANSFORMERS</u> <u>BOOSTERS</u> <u>FUSE</u>

F. -100V Peg

   1. Digit Resolver   36   Amp
   2. Address Gen.   ..45 Amp

         Total   36.45 Amp   4   Variac   5

Table 9.1 Continued
6.3 Volt Filament Loads

CHAPTER 10

TEST ROUTINES

A number of routines have been found to be particularly
useful in testing ORDVAC. These routines are of several different
kinds, designed to test for read-around ratio, memory flaws, adder
and digit resolver failures, and as overall tests of the machine's
operating condition. They are described in the following sections
of this chapter.

10.1 THE READ-AROUND ROUTINE. This test determines the
read-around ratio at each of the 1024 memory locations and prints
out which points have a read-around ratio less than a specified
number. The read-around ratio at a point is defined as the number
of times reference may be made to the point without affecting
neighboring points. It has been found that in the ORDVAC the greatest
difficulty is encountered when the point being referred to is a dash
and the neighboring points are dots.

The arrangement of memory locations in the ORDVAC memory
is such that the points form hexagons; thus except along the edges
each point is surrounded by 6 other points. The read-around test
takes each point in turn, surrounds it with dots and then writes
a dash n times in succession into the middle point. The surrounding
points are then tested and if any have turned to dashes a number
is printed out. The 10 digits of a printed number define the following quantities:

215

Input read around test number. Print it.

Start at first spot.

Surround spot by ones. Send zeros to spot at 8 per cycle and then at 1 per cycle.

Test surrounding spots.

Form the print base number, that is, the direction and address.

Print

Test in turn the digits of the number that failed.

Put tube number in print number. Print every 3 times.

Stop

Flip routine into other half of memory.

Arrange to test the next spot.

Start

Memory fully tested

First half tested

Half memory not fully tested

Half memory fully tested

End of test

Failure

Resume test

End

Failure

Resume test

READ AROUND BLOCK DIAGRAM

READ AROUND TEST

TAPE	MEMORY ADDRESS	DESCRIPTION	Page 1
80028 40001	0		
80028 40002	1		
24000 00000	2		
80028 40003	1		
28000 L5005	3		
80028 40004	1		
L4001 K0000	4	Special Bootstrap	
80028 40005	1		
00000 00001	5		
80028 40002	1		
22003 L0005	2		
28000 L5005	3		
L4001 K0000	4		
00000 00002	5		
80000 00000		Directive to 2F	
80028 4002F	1	Following words to 2F, etc.	

217

TAPE	MEMORY ADDRESS	DESCRIPTION	Page 2
00200 00200	2F		
00000 00000	30		
003LL 003LL	32	——— Address of x, point being tested	
00001 00001	34	——— Unit	
00020 00000	36		
00000 00001	38		
00000 00008	3K		
00000 00028	3N	——— Units for tube count	
10000 00000	3F		
80000 00000			
80028 40005	1	Directive to 5	
00000 00001	5		
80000 00000			
80028 40060	1	Directive to 60	
80028 40030	60		
F0830 80828	61	Read n from tape and print.	

READ AROUND TEST

TAPE	MEMORY ADDRESS	DESCRIPTION	Page 3
24064 00000	62	Read Around Protection	
00000 00000	63		
L5032 420S1	64		
460KS 420KS	65	Set address x in orders	
L50KS 400KK	66		
400KN 400KJ	67		
L5032 L4034	68	$x_1 = x + 1$	
460K1 L5032	69		
L0034 460K4	6K	$x_4 = x - 1$	
L5032 0000J	6S	Test if odd or even row	
K086F 28075	6N		
00000 00000	6J	Read around protection	
L5032 L0036	6F	$x_2 = x - 32$	
460K2 L0034	6L		
460K3 L5032	70	$x_3 = x - 33$	Odd Row
L4036 460K6	71	$x_6 = x + 32$	

219

TAPE	MEMORY ADDRESS	DESCRIPTION	Page 4
L0034 460K5	72	$x_5 = x + 31$	
L1038 240K1	73		
00000 00000	74	Read around protection	
L5032 L0036	75	$x_3 = x - 32$	
460K3 L4034	76	$x_2 = x - 31$	
460K2 L4036	77		
L4036 460K6	78	$x_6 = x + 33$	
L0034 K0072	79	$x_5 = x + 32$	
00000 00000	7K	Read around protection	
L5069 K00S5	7S		
80000 00000	7N	Directive to K1	
80028 400K1	7J		
40000 10001	K1		
40000 10001	K2	Set ones in x_i,	
40000 10001	K3	$i = 1, 2, \ldots 6$	
40000 10001	K4		

READ AROUND TEST

TAPE	MEMORY ADDRESS	DESCRIPTION	Page 5
40000 10001	K5	Set ones in x_i	
40000 L5030	K6	$i = 1, 2, \ldots 6$	
40020 240KF	K7	Set n in 20	
00000 00000	K8	Read around protection	
00000 40020	K9		
41000 41000	KK		
41000 41000	KS		Send 0's
00000 00000	KN	0's to x 8 times in sequence	to x 8 at a
00000 00000	KJ		cycle
L5020 L003K	KF	Reduce n by 8	
220K9 240S2	KL	Test n	
00000 00000	S0	Read around protection	
40020 41000	S1		Send 0's
L5020 L0038	S2	Reduce n by 1	to x 1 at a
28081 2407S	S3	Test when 0	cycle
00000 00000	S4	Read around protection	

221

TAPE	MEMORY ADDRESS	DESCRIPTION Page 6
L412K 46086	S5	Test x_i to determine failures
L5000 46087	S6	
F0800 L5038	S7'	
328SN 280S9	S8	
L5086 L0129	S9	
280FK 240S5	SK	
00000 00000	SS	Read around protection
358SJ 40022	SN	Plant failed number in 22,
L5086 L012S	SJ	Calculate direction of failure, put print base number in 26
0000N L4032	SF	
10014 24130	SL	
80000 00000		Directive to 130
80028 40130	1	
00008 40026	130	
40028 41020	131	
K0137 00000	132	

TAPE	MEMORY ADDRESS	DESCRIPTION Page 7
00000 00000	133	——— Read around protection
40022 40022	134	
L5020 L4038	135	
40020 L003N	136	— Calculate tube number
2813K L5022	137	
K00F0 K0934	138	
00000 00000	139	——— Read around protection
L5028 L003F	13K	Test if print number is full. If it is, print; if it is not, shift left 8 places.
280F0 00008	13S	
L003F 280S9	13N	
F0836 00027	13J	
80828 240S9	13F	— Print
80000 00000		
80028 400F0	1	— Directive to F0
F0000 40022	F0	
L5028 L4020	F1	

READ AROUND TEST

TAPE	MEMORY ADDRESS	DESCRIPTION
L003F 280F6	F2	If there are 3 values, print; otherwise shift 8 places with new tube number on the end.
L403F 00008	F3	
40028 24135	F4	
00000 00000	F5	Read around protection
F0836 00027	F6	
80828 L5026	F7	Print
40028 24135	F8	
00000 00000	F9	Read around protection
L5034 L4032	FK	Increase x modulo 1024
42032 46032	FS	
41020 L5032	FN	
00001 46020	FJ	Test to see of x = 0 modulo 512
L1020 2812N	FF	
24064 00000	FL	Positive test for next x value
00000 00000	LO	Read around protection
L5000 40200	L1	

224

TAPE	MEMORY ADDRESS	DESCRIPTION Page 9
L402F 46200	L2	
40020 42200	L3	
L50L1 L4034	L4	
460L1 420L1	L5	Shift numbers with variable addresses
42012 420L3	L6	
L00L9 280LS	L7	
280LS 00000	L8	
L5000 40200	L9	Constant
00000 00000	LK	Read around protection
L502F 4022F	LS	
L5030 40230	LN	Shift fixed number to other half of memory.
L5034 40234	LJ	
24120 00000	LF	
80000 00000		
80028 40120	1	Directive to 120
L5036 40236	120	

READ AROUND TEST

TAPE	MEMORY ADDRESS	DESCRIPTION	Page 10
L5038 40238	121		
L503K 4023K	122		
L503N 4023N	123	Shift fixed numbers to other half of memory.	
L503F 4023F	124		
L5032 40232	125		
L0038 28264	126		
30260 00004	127		
00000 00000	128	Read around protection	
L50K6 460S7	129		
L50K7 460S7	12K		
L509L 460S7	12S		
L512J 240L5	12N		
L5000 40200	12J		
80000 00000			
240FK 00000		Directive to 0.	

The first digit indicates at which of the 6 surrounding points of the hexagon the failure occurred. The next three digits give in sexadecimal notation the addresses of the point being bombarded when the failure occurred, and the following pairs of digits give in sexadecimal notation the numbers of the memory tubes upon which the failure occurred.

In order to test the entire memory, the routine flips itself alternately between the upper and lower halves of the memory. The routine is so designed that it will work with a read-around ratio as low as 2.

The number n is specified by a word on the input tape. The routine reads the tape and prints the number n as a 10 digit sexadecimal number. When the entire memory has been tested the routine will stop, and on being restarted, it will repeat the previous performance with the new value of n. It is recommended that the values of any given n be repeated due to the random fluctuations in the read-around ratio.

10.2 <u>STRIPES FLAW TEST.</u> This routine writes dashes on a field of dots, leaves them for about half a second and then tests to verify that the dashes have remained unaltered. When no flaws are found the monitor tube exhibits rows of stripes. When a flaw is found, the machine stops and the right hand address of R_3 gives the address of the flaw. The R_2 register contains the word which should have been written at this address while R_1 contains the contents of R_2 minus the word which was found at that address, i.e. if

227

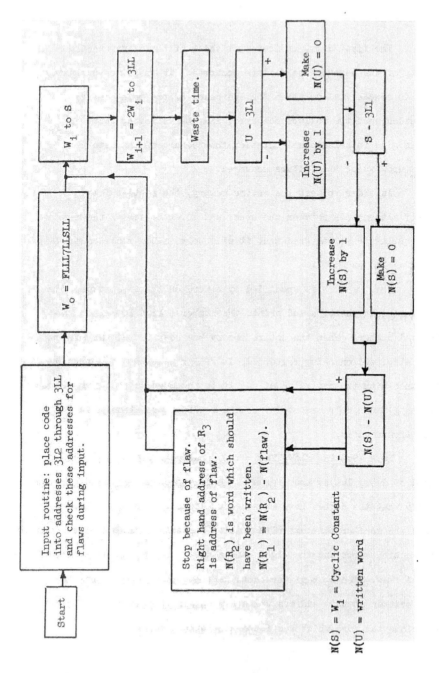

BLOCK DIAGRAM OF STRIPES FLAW TEST

$N(S) = W_1 = $ Cyclic Constant

$N(U) = $ written word

228

STRIPES FLAW TEST

TAPE	MEMORY ADDRESS	DESCRIPTION	Page 1
80028 40001	0		
80028 40002	1		
19026 24000	2	Bootstrap input	
80028 40000	1		
L4001 40001	0		
80028 403LL	1		
413L2 413L4	0		
413L6 413L8	0		
413LK 413LN	0	Write dashes and stop.	
413LF 30001	0		
L5200 403L2	0		
L5200 403L4	0		
L5200 403L6	0		
L5200 403L8	0	Restore dots.	
L5200 403LK	0		
L5200 403LN	0		

TAPE	MEMORY ADDRESS	DESCRIPTION Page 2
L5200 403LF	0	Restore dots.
413L3 413L5	0	
413L7 413L9	0	
413LS 413LJ	0	Write dashes in the other positions and stop.
413LL 30001	0	
L4001 40001	0	
80028 403L1	1	Bootstrap constant
35SL3 403L1	3L2	
KOSL4 403LL	3L3	Move cyclic number one place left and store.
0003L 0003L	3L4	Waste time.
FOSLL L53LS	3L5	
LO3LF 223L7	3L6	Replace cyclic number in R_2. Increase address in 3LS by 1 or make it 0.
L43L8 423LS	3L7	
L53LJ LO3L2	3L8	
283LK L43L8	3L9	Increase address in 3LJ by 1 or make it 0.
423LJ KO3LS	3LK	Control to right side of 3LS.

230

STRIPES FLAW TEST

TAPE	MEMORY ADDRESS	DESCRIPTION Page 3
303LJ L1000	3LS	Compare written word with cyclic word and continue or stop.
34SLS 283LJ	3LN	
35SL3 40208	3LJ	Store cyclic word at S.
303LJ L13L1	3LF	Comparison constant
FLLL7 LLSLL	3LL	Cyclic constant
FOSLL 243LJ	0	Transfer control with R_2 containing the sequence 12 1's, 0; 12 1's; 12 1's, 0.

there are m ones in the R_1 register then the flaw was in tube
m-1.

      To check the storage locations wherein the test is being
placed, alternate 0's and 1's are written there during input.
The machine will stop twice while a visual check is being made
of the 40 monitor tubes.

      10.3 <u>THE DYNAMIC ADDER - DIGIT RESOLVER TEST.</u> The dy-
namic adder - digit resolver routine is a test routine for detect-
ing transient malfunctions in the adder and digit resolver. The
routine is diagnostic to the extent that printed results indicate
that digit of the forty digits in which the malfunction occurs.
Four tests are executed in sequence, each test consisting of six
additions. The tests are as follows:

ROW	<u>A</u> +555 Test	<u>B</u> +KKK Test	<u>C</u> -KKK Test	<u>D</u> -555 Test
	LLLLL	LLLLL	LLLLL	LLLLL
(1)	<u>+55556</u>	<u>+KKKKS</u>	<u>-KKKKK</u>	<u>-55555</u>
	55555	KKKKK	55555	KKKKK
(2)	<u>+00001</u>	<u>+00001</u>	<u>-LLLLL</u>	<u>-LLLLL</u>
	55556	KKKKS	55556	KKKKS
(3)	<u>+LLLLL</u>	<u>+LLLLL</u>	<u>-00001</u>	<u>-00001</u>
	55555	KKKKK	55555	KKKKK
(4)	<u>+55555</u>	<u>+KKKKS</u>	<u>-KKKKS</u>	<u>-55555</u>
	KKKKK	55555	KKKKK	55555

(5)	+55555	+KKKKK	-KKKKS	-55556
(X)	LLLLL	LLLLL	LLLLL	LLLLL
(6)	+00001	+00001	-LLLLL	-LLLLL
(Y)	00000	00000	00000	00000

Tests A and C and tests B and D produce identical input signals
to the adder and digit resolver; the test pairs differ in the setting of the complement gate. If a test is executed correctly, the
quantity in row (X) will be negative and the quantity in row (Y)
will be positive; otherwise a mark indicative of failure is stored
in the memory. If, after one set of four tests, any failure has
been indicated the quantities of row (X) are printed. Counting
routines are provided with the result that a conditional stop is
encountered after either (a) 8000 sets of tests have been executed (1 minute, 30 seconds), (b) 9 sets of printings of four
words each have occurred. The counting routines do not use the
adder or digit resolver circuits.

Input Information. The tape supplied incorporates a bootstrap routine starting at address 0. The routine may also be put
into the machine with order pairs by the following procedure:
(a) The twelfth tape word (the second 00000 00000) is inserted at
successive addresses 41 through 5N. (b) The next tape word
(7LLLL LL080) is a key word and need not be read in. (c) The
following tape word (F92LL 10027) is inserted at address 80 and
the remaining words on the tape, with the exception of the last

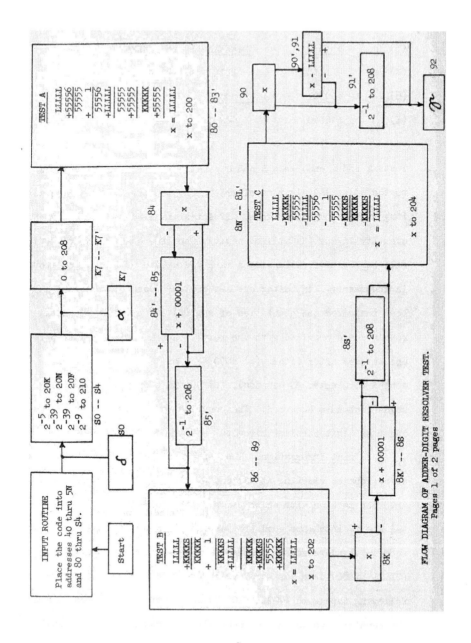

FLOW DIAGRAM OF ADDER-DIGIT RESOLVER TEST.
Pages 1 of 2 pages

234

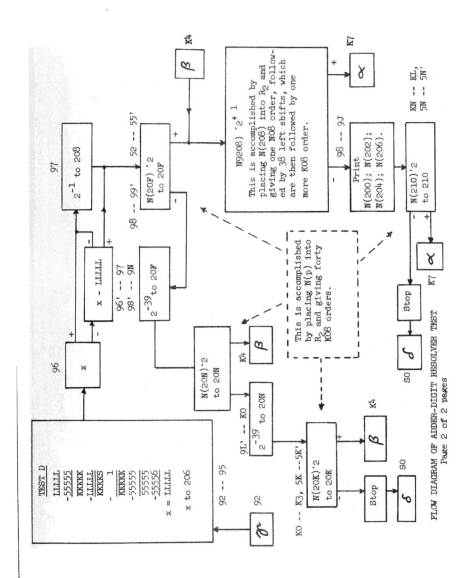

FLOW DIAGRAM OF ADDER-DIGIT RESOLVER TEST
Page 2 of 2 pages

235

ADDER DIGIT RESOLVER TEST

TAPE	MEMORY ADDRESS	DESCRIPTION Page 1
80028 40001	0	This program has an input routine which is different from the bootstrap routine which is usually used.
80028 40002	1	
L5001 30800	2	
80028 40000	1	Input routine
42001 80028	0	
00000 00000		Immaterial
28003 40002	1	Beyond here the input routine must have orders which are negative numbers.
L4005 28000	3	
L0005 K0001	4	
80000 01000	5	
7LLLL LL040		Key word
00000 00000	40	
LLLLL LLLLL	41	
00000 00001	42	Constants
LLLLL LLLLL	43	
55555 55555	44	

ADDER DIGIT RESOLVER TEST

TAPE	MEMORY ADDRESS	DESCRIPTION	Page 2
LLLLL LLLLL	45		
55555 55556	46		
LLLLL LLLLL	47		
LLLLL LLLLL	48		
KKKKK KKKKK	49		
LLLLL LLLLL	4K		
KKKKK KKKKS	4S	←── Constants	
LLLLL LLLLL	4N		
LLLLL LLLLL	4J		
LLLLL LLLLL	4F		
LLLLL LLLLL	4L		
LLLLL LLLLL	50		
LLLLL LLLLL	51		
K0853 K0853	52		
K089K 28054	53	←── Shifting routine for least significant digit count	
K0855 K0855	54		
K089K 28052	55		

237

ADDER DIGIT RESOLVER TEST

TAPE	MEMORY ADDRESS	DESCRIPTION Page 3
LLLLL LLLLL	56	
K0858 K0858	57	Shifting routine for second digit count
K089F 28057	58	
LLLLL LLLLL	59	
K08K2 2805K	5K	Shifting routine for most significant digit count
LLLLL LLLLL	5S	
K08KF 2805N	5N	Shifting routine for print count
7LLLL LL080	5J	Key word for input routine
F92LL 10027	80	
L4046 L4042	81	
L404L L4044	82	
L4044 40200	83	+ 555 test
22085 L4042	84	
28086 49208	85	
F92LL 10027	86	+ KKK test
L404S L4042	87	

238

ADDER DIGIT RESOLVER TEST

TAPE	MEMORY ADDRESS	DESCRIPTION	Page 4
L404L L404S	88		
L4049 40202	89	+ KKK test	
2208S L4042	8K		
2808N 49208	8S		
F92LL 10027	8N		
L0049 L004L	8J		
L0042 L004S	8F	- KKK test	
L004S 40204	8L		
22091 L004L	90		
28092 49028	91		
F92LL 10027	92		
L0044 L004L	93	- 555 test	
L0042 L0044	94		
L0046 40206	95		
22097 L004L	96		
28098 49208	97		

239

ADDER DIGIT RESOLVER TEST

TAPE	MEMORY ADDRESS	DESCRIPTION Page 5
19026 FOKOF	98	
24052 30099	99	Least significant digit count
K089S 4020F	9K	
280K4 19026	9S	
4020F FOKON	9N	Reset least significant digit counter and count in second digit
24057 3009J	9J	
K089L 4020N	9F	
280K4 19026	9L	
4020N FOKOK	K0	
2405K 300K1	K1	Reset second digit counter and count in most significant digit
K08K3 4020K	K2	
280K4 300S0	K3	Stop after 1 minute 30 seconds.
FOKO8 K08K5	K4	If any failures have occurred, $2^{-1}R = 1$, $2^{-39}R = 1$, $2^{-1}R_1 = 1$, $2^0 R_1 = 1$.
00026 K08K6	K5	
280K7 240K8	K6	
41208 24080	K7	Repeat test if no failures

ADDER DIGIT RESOLVER TEST

TAPE	MEMORY ADDRESS	DESCRIPTION	Page 6
FOK00 80828	K8		
FOK02 80828	K9		
FOK04 80828	KK	Print results of 4 tests if error has occurred on 1 or more	
FOK06 80828	KS		
19026 FOK10	KN		
2405N 300KJ	KJ	Count in print counter	
K08KL 40210	KF		
280K7 30080	KL	Stops after 9 sets of prints	
19004 4020K	S0		
19026 4020N	S1	Set test counter	
19026 4020F	S2		
19008 40210	S3		
240K7 00000	S4		
7LLLL LL000		Key word for input routine	
24080 00000	00	Transfers control from input routine to main routine	

two, are inserted in successive addresses. The third from last word should be inserted in address 54. The last two tape words are associated with the bootstrap input routine. (d) To begin the routine, transfer control to address OSO.

10.4 THE LEAPFROG TEST. This test was designed to verify that all parts of the ORDVAC are working correctly under dynamic working conditions. The routine consists essentially of three tests, a multiplication test, a division test, and a summation test. The routine displaces itself in the memory by copying itself and transferring control to the new copy. While this is being done the sum of routine is formed and this should be a zero. When the machine is working properly zero will be printed every ten minutes, apart from the first number printed.

Multiplication Test. This is performed using an exact arithmetic identity.

If we multiply a x b and a x (-b) and add together the most significant and least significant halves of the double length products the results should be -1, any single error invalidating this result. The two multiplications that are necessary are done by different variants of the multiplication order, in one case the rounded multiplication order being used while in the other case the held multiplication order is used. The intermediate results of this test are used to generate the sequence of random numbers a and b, used in the multiplication and division tests.

Failure of the multiplication test is recognized by the

242

LEAPFROG BLOCK DIAGRAM

243

LEAPFROG ROUTINE

TAPE	MEMORY ADDRESS	DESCRIPTION Page 1
FOL40 7J741	3N0	This routine should be preceded by a bootstrap start.
34LN2 40701	3N1	
L1741 40702	3N2	
L57L1 FOL02	3N3	Multiplication test
74740 34LN5	3N4	
L4701 40742	3N5	
L7742 287J0	3N6	-R$_1$ should be -1
L7740 L2741	3N7	Test whether to interchange a, b.
287J3 L5740	3N8	
66741 40743	3N9	Residue
35LNS 287NN	3NK	Test if quotient is + or - .
		Division Test
L5741 KO7NN	3NS	
L1741 L4743	3NN	Remainder
74741 LO740	3NJ	
40744 L3744	3NF	Form test number
32LJ0 287J6	3NL	If R$_1$ positive do not print

244

TAPE	MEMORY ADDRESS	DESCRIPTION Page 2
40745 FOL45	3J0	
80828 00001	3J1	Print test number when not correct
307J0 K17F4	3J2	Return to repeat test
L5740 FOL41	3J3	
40741 35LJ5	3J4	Interchange divisor and dividend
40740 247N7	3J5	
L57N0 40746	3J6	
40747 40748	3J7	Waste Order
00008 F0000	3J8	Examine 9th digit of word
227JJ L5746	3J9	
L07FF 42746	3JK	
46746 L5747	3JS	Increase address of word if necessary
L0748 46747	3JN	
42747 L5746	3JJ	
40749 40781	3JF	Transfer modified word
L5747 L474K	3JL	Sum check

LEAPFROG ROUTINE

TAPE	MEMORY ADDRESS	DESCRIPTION	Page 3
10018 1000L	3F0	Form sum check mod $1 - 2^{-39}$	
34LF2 4074K	3F1	using right shift order to test shift counter.	
L5701 40741	3F2		
L5702 40740	3F3	Plant new random numbers	
L57FJ L4748	3F4		
4274S 4674S	3F5	Adjust transfer addresses	
467J6 427JF	3F6		
247N0 4274S	3F7		
L57F3 L07F2	3F8	Test if origin is reached	
287FS F0L89	3F9		
80828 00001	3FK	Is so, print old sum	
4174K L3789	3FS	Clear new sum Test last sum	
227F4 307J0	3FN	Resume test if positive	
J0001 00001	3FJ	Unit address increment	
0003L 0003L	3FF	Address increment	
00003 00003	3FL	Waste order	

LEAPFROG ROUTINE

TAPE	MEMORY ADDRESS	DESCRIPTION Page 4
007N0 00781	3L0	—————— Starting constant
40000 00000	3L1	
12345 6789K	3L2	
LFJNS K2584	3L3	—— Two primary "random" numbers
L5312 40340	3L4	
L53L3 40341	3L5	
L53L0 L03LF	3L6	—— Wasteful starting procedures
4174S L57L0	3L7	
4674S K07F7	3L8	
00000 00000	3L9	
S5S81 2613F	3LK	
03000 00000	3LS	
00000 00000	3LN	—— Waste
00000 00000	3LJ	
00000 00000	3LF	
L57L0 247L7	3LL	—— This will overwrite first word of old copy when transfer is finished and transfer control to new sum.
243L4 00001	00	—— Overwrite bootstrap and start.

247

machine's printing a positive number, and stopping.

Division Test. The division is checked by a multiplication and the final result should be the dividend exactly. The formula used is:

Dividend = quotient x divisor + remainder

To use this formula it is necessary to ensure (by interchanging if necessary) that the divisor is greater than the dividend. It is also necessary to compute the remainder from the residue left in the R_1 register at the end of a division.

Failure of the division test is recognized by the machine's printing a negative number and stopping.

Failure of the sum test is recognized by the machine's stopping before printing a negative number.

If the multiplication test fails, the orders should be obeyed one by one until an FON order appears as the left hand order in R_3. The succeeding orders can be obeyed one at a time, the store orders (40) being replaced by hold subtract (LO) with the same address. This will determine which part of the multiplication test fails, if the second run is correct.

If the division test failed, then the orders of this should be repeated one by one in a similar fashion.

10.5 THE CRIPPLED LEAPFROG TEST ROUTINE. The crippled leapfrog test routine consists essentially of the multiplication test, division test and random number generations routine of the leapfrog

CRIPPLED LEAPFROG ROUTINE

TAPE	MEMORY ADDRESS	DESCRIPTION Page 1
80028 40001	0	
80028 40002	1	
19026 24000	2	Bootstrap input
80028 40000	1	
L4001 42001	0	
80028 403N3	1	
40000 00000	3N4	1/2
FOSJJ 7J3JL	3N5	
40202 34SN7	3N6	First half of multiplication test
40204 L13JL	3N7	
40200 L53N4	3N8	
FOK00 743JJ	3N9	
40206 34SNS	3NK	Second half of multiplication test
40208 L4204	3NS	
4020K L720K	3NN	To mult. print routine -1 in R_1 if correct
283F0 L73JJ	3NJ	Check relative absolute values of a, b.
L23JL 283J9	3NF	To interchange of a, b.

249

CRIPPLED LEAFFROG ROUTINE

TAPE	MEMORY ADDRESS	DESCRIPTION	Page 2
L53JJ 663JL	3NL		
4020N 35SJ1	3J0	Divide and store residue and quotient	
40212 283J3	3J1		
L53JL K03J3	3J2		
L13JL L420N	3J3	Form remainder	
40214 743JL	3J4	Remainder	
40210 L03JJ	3J5	a/b x b	
4020F L320F	3J6		
328J8 40216	3J7		
283L8 243FN	3J8	Store new a, b / To divide print routine	
L53JJ FOSJL	3J9		
403JL 35SJS	3JK	Interchange a, b	
403JJ 243NL	3JS		
LLLLL LLLLL	3JN	Read around isolation	
12345 6789K	3JJ	a	
LLLLL LLLLL	3JF	Read around isolation	
LFJNS K2584	3JL	b	

CRIPPLED LEAPFROG ROUTINE

TAPE	MEMORY ADDRESS	DESCRIPTION	Page 3
FOSJJ 80828	3F0		
FOKO2 80828	3F1	—a x b, rounded, first half	
FOKO4 80828	3F2	—First half + second half	
FOSN4 80828	3F3		
FOSJL 80828	3F4	Print results of multiplication test	
FOKO6 80828	3F5	--b x a, holding, first half	
FOKO8 80828	3F6	—First half + second half	
FOKOK 80828	3F7	---1 if correct	
L53NJ FOSFS	3F8		
403FS 35SFK	3F9	Interchange conditional and unconditional transfers to multiplication print routine	
403NJ 243N5	3FK		
243FO 00000	3FS	Temporary storage for transfer order to multiplication print routine	
FOSJJ 80828	3FN	—a, dividend	
FOSJL 80828	3FJ	—b, divisor Print results of division test	
FOKON 80828	3FF	—d, residue	
FOKOF 80828	3FL	—e = (a + b) x b - a (first half)	

CRIPPLED LEAPFROG ROUTINE

TAPE	MEMORY ADDRESS	DESCRIPTION Page 4
FOK10 80828	3L0	— (a + b) x b, first half
FOK12 80828	3L1	— quotient
		Print results of division test
FOK14 80828	3L2	— Remainder
FOK16 80282	3L3	Negative absolute value of first half + second half of (a + b) x b - a.
L53J8 FOSL7	3L4	
403L7 358L6	3L5	Interchange conditional and unconditional transfers to division print routine
403J8 K03NJ	3L6	— To division test
243FN 00000	3L7	Temporary storage for transfer order to division print routine
L5204 403JL	3L8	
L5200 403JJ	3L9	— Store new a, b
243N5 00000	3LK	
LLLLL LLLLL	3LS	
LLLLL LLLLL	3LN	
LLLLL LLLLL	3LJ	— Read around isolation
LLLLL LLLLL	3LF	
LLLLL LLLLL	3LL	
243N5 00000	00	— Bootstrap input constant

252

routine. The crippled leapfrog differs from the leapfrog in that the orders remain in fixed locations in the memory and intermediate results of the multiplication and division tests are retained. For transient errors, both an incorrect and correct copy of the test results will usually be printed.

Printed Results. Separate routines are used for printing results of the multiplication and division tests. In each case, eight results of an incorrect calculation are printed, followed by eight corresponding results of the same calculation repeated. For transient malfunctions, the second set of results is usually correct. Results are printed in the following order:

MULTIPLICATION TEST

1. a
2. First half of product a b
3. Sum of halves of product a b
4. Stored constant 1/2
5. b
6. First half of product -ba
7. Sum of halves of product -ba
8. Sum of half-product sums ab + (-ba)

DIVISION TEST

1. Dividend a
2. Divisor b
3. Residue d
4. a/b x b - a
5. a/b x b (first half)
6. Quotient a/b
7. Remainder
8. $-\left|\text{first half } a/b \text{ x } b - a\right|$
   $-\left|\text{second half } a/b \text{ x } b\right|$

253

10.6 **THE FINAL TEST ROUTINE.** This program was designed to give an over-all test to ORDVAC and was one of the routines used in the final acceptance tests. This program generates a set of 352 pseudo-random numbers b_i and stores them in successive memory positions B_i. It then performs multiplications and divisions of b_i by b_{i+1}, checking multiplication results by multiplying in both directions and checking division results by multiplying. If all of these are correct, the numbers are transferred to 352 other locations and the transfers are checked. If there is no failure, the process is repeated but on the transfer the numbers are each shifted one place thus utilizing different storage locations for each of the numbers. After 16 of these small cycles, the machine prints a number, counting in the sexadecimal system from a starting value of 1L0 and it takes 22 print cycles to run through the 352 numbers. This is a large cycle. After 16 large cycles (about 8 1/2 hours) the machine will reach an unconditional stop and must be started again.

Table 10.1 lists some of the operations carried out during 1 print cycle (about 81 seconds).

ORDER	NUMBER IN ONE PRINT CYCLE
Order Pairs	239,568
Multiplications	22,528
Divisions	5,632
Additions	203,028
Single shifts	1,492,608
Printings	1

Table 10.1 Operations During One Print Cycle

If there is a failure, the machine will stop. Upon being started again it will print the addresses B_i and B_{i+1} involved in the computation and stop. Upon being started again it will print the computations which disagreed and stop once more. Then upon being started it will enter a subroutine which systematically checks the major orders of the order code and stops if failures occur.

The program is written so that the contents of R_3 at a stop reveal the cause of the stop. These stops (all type 30 conditional stops except the 8 1/2 hour programmed stop, which is a 20 stop) are given in Table 10.2.

CONTENTS OF R_3

3 0 0 8 N L 5 0 0 J	$b_j \times b_{j+1}$ vs $b_{j+1} \times b_j$, rounded
3 0 0 8 N L 5 0 1 2	$b_j \times b_{j+1}$, rounded vs unrounded
3 0 0 8 N L 5 0 2 2	$(b_{j+1} + b_j) \times b_j$
3 0 0 9 7 L 5 0 2 8	$B_{j+k} > 1024$
3 0 0 9 9 L 5 0 3 1	$j > 160$ꈜ during transfer
3 0 0 9 1 L 5 0 4 4	$b_j \neq b_{j+k}$. Transfer failure
2 4 0 3 S 3 0 0 3 S	Failure of 24 order
3 0 0 9 S L 5 0 3 K	$B_j > 1024$
3 0 0 9 J L 5 0 4 K	$j > 160$ during transfer check
3 0 0 9 L L 5 0 5 4	$K > 2$ NO

ꈜ160 sexadecimal $= 352$ decimal

Table 10.2 Failures in Final Test
Routine

255

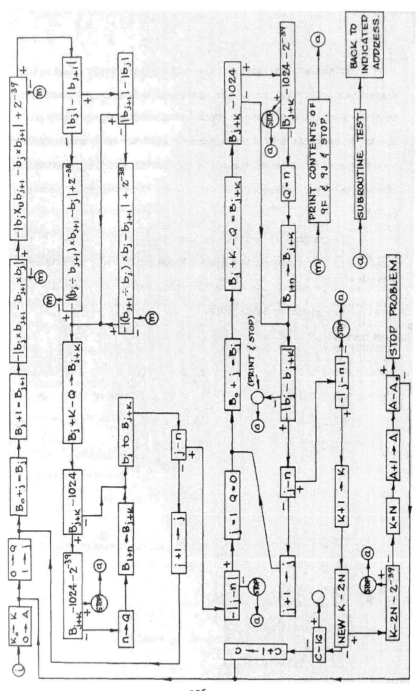

FINAL TEST ROUTINE FLOW DIAGRAM

256

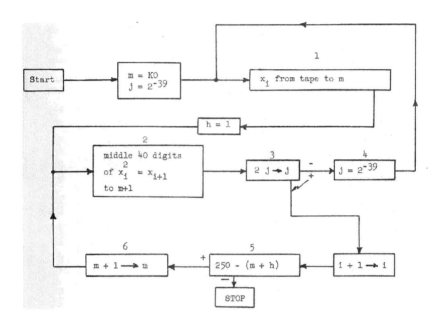

Start → m = KO, j = 2^{-39}

1
x_i from tape to m

h = 1

2
middle 40 digits
of x_i^2 = x_{i+1}
to m+1

3
2 j → j

4
j = 2^{-39}

6
m + 1 ⟶ m

5
250 - (m + h)

STOP

i + 1 ⟶ i

FINAL TEST ROUTINE - RANDOM NUMBERS BLOCK DIAGRAM

257

TAPE	MEMORY ADDRESS	DESCRIPTION	Page 1
80028 40001	0		
80028 40002	1		
19026 24000	2	Bootstrap	
80028 40000	1		
L4001 42001	0		
80028 403F8	1		
80028 40000	3F9		
19026 L43F9	3FK		
403F9 L03FJ	3FS	Input Test Routine	
283FF 243F9	3FN		
80028 400K4	3FJ		
80028 400N3	3FF		
19025 L43FF	3FL		
403FF L03L2	3L0	Input Constants	
283LL 243FF	3L1		
80028 400J9	3L2		
19026 4000J	3L3	Set counter 2^{-39}	

FINAL TEST ROUTINE

TAPE	MEMORY ADDRESS	DESCRIPTION Page 2
80028 4001L	3L4	Store word from tape in 1L
F081L 7501L	3L5	
10014 35SL7	3L6	Square and put middle digits in 1L
F03LK 4001L	3L7	
40140 L500J	3L8	
F03L9 4000J	3L9	Count 1 to 39
283LS 243L3	3LK	
19012 L43L8	3LS	Increase storing address by 1
403L8 L03LF	3LN	
283F9 243L5	3LJ	Test for end
402K0 L500J	3LF	Constant for end test
K03LL 30000	3LL	Stop before starting problem
243L3 00000	0	Stop inputting

The words 3L4 to 3LL constitute the routine for generating the
352 random numbers. The next 10 words on the tape are numbers
used as starting values for the random numbers.

TAPE	MEMORY ADDRESS	DESCRIPTION	Page 3
L50NJ 400JS	0	K = 1F0 to JS A = 0 to JJ	
410JJ 410J1	1	Q = 0 to J1	
L50N7 400N5	2	j = 1 to N5	
L40NL 400J9	3	$B_0 + j = B_j$ to J9	
4602S 46006	4	Plant B_j in 2S and 6	
L40N7 46007	5	Plant B_{j+1} in 7	
L5000 400JL	6	b_j to JL	
L5000 40100	7	b_{j+1} to 100	
F0900 7J0JL	8	$b_{j+1} \times b_j$ to 102	
40102 F08JL	9		
7J100 40104	K	$b_j \times b_{j+1}$ to 104	
L0102 40106	S	Test $-\left| b_j \times b_{j+1} - b_{j+1} \times b_j \right|$	
L3106 2800F	N	To F if $b_j \times b_{j+1} = b_{j+1} \times b_j$	
3008N L500J	J	To print and stop routine (rounded mult. failure)	
F08JL 75100	F	$b_j \; X_u \; b_{j+1}$ to 102	
40102 L0104	L		
		The words in 8 through J test multiplication.	

260

FINAL TEST ROUTINE

TAPE	MEMORY ADDRESS	DESCRIPTION Page 4
40106 19026	10	Test $-\left\| b_j \; X_u \; b_{j+1} = b_j \times b_{j+1} \right\| + 2^{-39}$
L2106 28013	11	To 13 if $b_j \; X_u \; b_{j+1} \approx b_j \times b_{j+1}$
3008N L5012	12	To print and stop routine
L70JL L2100	13	$\left\| b_j \right\| - \left\| b_{j+1} \right\|$ to R_1.
2801S L50JL	14	To 1S if $\left\| b_j \right\| \geq \left\| b_{j+1} \right\|$.
40104 66100	15	b_j to 104
7J100 40102	16	$(b_j + b_{j+1}) \times b_{j+1}$ to 102
L00JL 40106	17	$-\left\| (b_j + b_{j+1}) \times b_{j+1} - b_j \right\| + 2^{-38}$
19025 L2106	18	
28023 24022	19	To 23 if ≥ 0 To 22 if < 0
L5000 L0000	1K	Wasted word
L7100 L20JL	1S	$\left\| b_{j+1} \right\| - \left\| b_j \right\|$ to R_1
28023 L5100	1N	To 23 if $\left\| b_{j+1} \right\| \geq \left\| b_j \right\|$
40104 660JL	1J	b_{j+1} to 104
7J0JL 40102	1F	$(b_{j+1} + b_j) \times b_j$ to 102
L0100 40106	1L	Words 14-20 test multiplication against division.

261

TAPE	MEMORY ADDRESS	DESCRIPTION Page 5
19025 L2106	20	$-\left\lvert (b_{j+1} \dotplus b_j) \times b_j \dotminus b_{j+1} \right\rvert \dotplus 2^{-38}$
28023 24022	21	To 23 if ≥ 0 To 22 if < 0
3008N L5022	22	To print and stop routine
L50J9 L40JS	23	$B_j + K - Q = B_{j+k}$ to R_1
L00J1 4202S	24	Plant B_{j+k} in 2S
L00J3 22026	25	$B_{j+k} - 1024$ to R_1. To 26' when $B_{j+k} = 1024$
2402S L00J5	26	To 2S if $B_{j+k} < 1024$. $(B_{j+k} - 1024) - 2^{-39}$
28028 24029	27	To 28 if ≥ 0 To 29 if < 0
30097 L5028	28	Stop. To 97 (word at 2S is printed) and stop again.
L50N9 400J1	29	$Q = 1S0$ to J1
L50J7 4202S	2K	Plant B_{1+k} in 2S'
L5000 40000	2S	Transfer b_j to B_{j+k}
L50N5 L00N9	2N	j-n to 106
40106 28030	2J	To 30 if $j \geq n$.
L50N5 L40N7	2F	$j + 1 \longrightarrow j$ to N5.
400N5 24003	2L	To 3

TAPE	MEMORY ADDRESS	DESCRIPTION Page 6
L3106 28032	30	$- \lvert j - n \rvert$ to R_1
30099 L5031	31	Stop; then to 99, print j; stop again.
410J1 L50N7	32	$Q = 0$ to J1
400N5 L40NL	33	$j = 1$ to N5 $B_0 + j = B_j$ to R_1
4603J L40JS	34	Plant B_j in 3J $B_j + K - Q = B_{j+k}$ to R_1.
L00J1 4203J	35	Plant B_{j+k} in 3J'
L00J3 28038	36	$B_j - 1024$ in R_1 To 38 if $B_j \geq 1024$
240K2 2403J	37	To K2 where right shifts are performed to reduce RAR
L00J5 2803K	38	$B_j - 1024 - 2^{-39}$ to R . To 3K if ≥ 0
2403S 3003S	39	To 3S if < 0 Wasted order.
3009S L503K	3K	Stop; to 9S, print contents of 3J; stop again.
L50N9 400J1	3S	$Q = 160$ to J1
L50J7 4203J	3N	$B_1 + n \xrightarrow{} B_{j+k}$ Plant B_{j+k} in 3J'
L5000 L0000	3J	Compare b_j with b_{j+k}.
40106 L3106	3F	
28045 L503J	3L	To 45 if $- \lvert b_j - b_{j+k} \rvert \geq 0$

263

FINAL TEST ROUTINE

TAPE	MEMORY ADDRESS	DESCRIPTION Page 7
46041 42042	40	
F0800 80828	41	Print b_j and b_{j+k} They should agree.
K0042 K0800	42	Wasted Order.
80828 24044	43	Wasted Order.
30091 L5044	44	Stop; to 91, print addresses B_j and B_{j+k}, and stop again.
L50N5 L00N9	45	$(j-n)$ to 106
40106 28049	46	To 49 if $j \geq n$.
L50N7 L40N5	47	$j + 1 \longrightarrow j$ to N5
400N5 K0033	48	To 33'
L2106 2804S	49	$- \lvert j - n \rvert$ to R_1. To 4S if ≥ 0.
3009J L504K	4K	Stop; to subroutine when restarted.
L50JS L40N7	4S	$K + 1 \longrightarrow K$ to JS.
400JS L10N9	4N	New $K - 2_n$ to R_1.
L00N9 L40JS	4J	To 4L if $K \geq 2n$ To 55 if $K < 2n$
2804L 24055	4F	$K - 2n - 2^{-39}$ to R_1 To 54 if ≥ 0.
L00J5 28054	4L	

TAPE	MEMORY ADDRESS	DESCRIPTION $\qquad$ Page 8
L50N9 400JS	50	$K_0 = n_0$ at JS
L50N7 L40JJ	51	$A + 1 \longrightarrow A$ to JJ
400JJ L00N3	52	New $A - A_0$
2808S K0001	53	To FINAL PROBLEM STOP. Start new cycle at 1'.
3009L L5054	54	Fail stop; to 9L, print K; stop again.
L50N7 24093	55	Begin count for sub cycle (prints every 16th time) to 93.
K0056 L40N7	56	
4208S F0902	57	Print contents of 102 and 104 and stop for examination.
80828 F0904	58	
80828 3005S	59	
L40N7 4208S	5K	Plant proper address at 8S' before entering subroutine.
19001 2205N	5S	SUBROUTINE
3005J 2805F	5N	Test positive sensing of C and C'
3005F 3005F	5J	
F9000 28060	5F	
22060 24061	5L	Test negative sensing of C and C'.

265

FINAL TEST ROUTINE

TAPE	MEMORY ADDRESS	DESCRIPTION	Page 9
30061 30061	60		
L53LL LO3LL	61		
28063 30063	62	—— Fail stop	Test + and (-) orders.
LOOJ5 22064	63		
24065 30065	64	—— Fail stop	
L13LL L43LL	65		
28067 30067	66	—— Fail stop	Test - and (+) orders.
LOOJ5 22068	67		
24069 30069	68	—— Fail stop	
L73LL L23LL	69		
2806S 30068	6K	—— Fail stop	Test + and - orders.
LOOJ5 2206N	6S		
2406J 3006J	6N	—— Fail stop	
L33LL L63LL	6J		
2806L 3006L	6F	—— Fail stop	Test - and + orders.
LOOJ5 22070	6L		

TAPE	MEMORY ADDRESS	DESCRIPTION	Page 10
24071 30071	70	Fail stop	
FOSLL L53LL	71		
K0072 30874	72		
30074 30074	73	Test R and A (-).	
28075 30075	74		
L00J5 22076	75		
24077 30077	76	Fail stop	
FO8JS 80828	77	Print K	Normally occurs every 16th time. If a failure causes an entry into this subroutine, one or more Ks will appear alike which will indicate this fact.
19026 00001	78		
00025 F0000	79		
2807S K0073	7K	Test	
3007N 19001	7S	→→ 38 ← 1 ← 37	
1000K 0000S	7N	FO → 1 → 10 ← 11 →→ 37 ← 37	
F0000 2207F	7J		
2407L 3007L	7F		
19025 00025	7L		

FINAL TEST ROUTINE

TAPE	MEMORY ADDRESS	DESCRIPTION	Page 11
F0000 22081	80		
24082 30082	81		
L50J9 42083	82		
46084 L5000	83		
L0000 22085	84	Test E	
30086 L00J5	85	and E'	
28087 24088	86		
30088 30088	87		
24089 3008S	88		
K008S 3008S	89	Test U and U'	
3008S 3008S	8K		
20000 24000	8S	STOP PROBLEM. Return to subroutine LINK	
42090 L5006	8N		
46108 L5007	8J	Print addresses B_j and B_{j+1}	
10014 42108	8F	before printing errors in the computation which used contents	
F0908 80828	8L	of B_j and B_{j+1}.	

268

TAPE	MEMORY ADDRESS	DESCRIPTION Page 12
30056 L5000	90	
F083J 80828	91	Print word with address B_j
3005K L5044	92	and B_{j+k} after printing contents of $B_j + B_{j+k}$
L40K1 400K1	93	$C + 1 \rightarrow C$
L00N3 22095	94	$C - 16$ to 95' if 0
K0001 410K1	95	Begin new subcycle if < 0 $0 \rightarrow C$
L5094 K005K	96	To sub-routine
F082S 80828	97	Print word with address B_{j+k} in right half; stop, then to subroutine.
3005K L5028	98	
F08N5 80828	99	Print j and stop, then to subroutine (should not exceed 160).
3005K L5031	9K	
F083J 80828	9S	Print word with address B_{j+k} in right half and stop; then to subroutine.
3005K L503K	9N	
F08N5 80828	9J	Print j and stop (should not exceed 160) then to subroutine.
3005K L504K	9F	
F08JS 80828	9L	Print K

269

TAPE	MEMORY ADDRESS	DESCRIPTION Page 13
3005K L5054	K0	
00000 00000	K1	——— Temporary Storage
1003L 1003L	K2	
1003L K0037	K3	—— Correct for RAR
00010 00010	N3	——— $A_0 = (10)_{16}$ Thus the machine prints every 16th time and runs 16 large cycles of about 1/2 hour per cycle.
00000 00000	N5	
00001 00001	N7	
00160 00160	N9	——— $n = (160)_{16}$
00000 00002	NS	
001F0 001F0	NJ	——— $K_0 = (1F0)_{16}$
0013L 0013L	NL	——— $B_0 = (13L)_{16}$
00000 00000	J1	——— 0 or n
00400 00400	J3	$(1024)_{10}$
00000 00001	J5	
002K0 002K0	J7	——— $B_{1+n} = (2K0)_{16}$ End of tape
	J9	——— Temporary Storage

FINAL TEST ROUTINE

TAPE	MEMORY ADDRESS	DESCRIPTION Page 14
	JS	Temporary Storage. K increases by 1 each time and is printed every 16th time. Start at 1L0.
	JJ	
	JL	Temporary Storage
	100	
	102	Store two numbers to be printed out.
	104	
	106	Temporary Storage
	108	Addresses B_j and B_{j+1} are planted here to be printed out.

271

REFERENCES

1. Preliminary Discussion of the Logical Design of an Electronic Computing Instrument, Burks, Goldstine, von Neumann. Institute for Advanced Study (Princeton, N. J.), June 1946.

2. Planning and Coding of Problems for an Electronic Computing Instrument, Goldstine and von Neumann. Institute for Advanced Study, 1947.

3. A Storage System for Use with Binary-Digital Computing Machines, Williams, Kilburn, Proceedings of Institution of Electrical Engineers (London), vol. 96, part II, number 50, April 1949, pages 183-202.

4. Report on Input Output Transcribers Developed at the National Bureau of Standards for the Institute for Advanced Study Type of Computing Machine, A. Orden, L. Cahn and J. H. Wright, Number OD-10-8R National Bureau of Standards, March 1948.

5. Restoring and Non-restoring Division, J. E. Robertson, Internal Report Number 27, Electronic Digital Computer, University of Illinois, April 1951.

6. Interim Progress Report on the Physical Realization of an Electronic Computing Instrument, Bigelow, et al. Institute for Advanced Study, January 1947.

7. Second Interim Progress Report on the Physical Realization of an Electronic Computing Instrument, Bigelow, et al. Institute for Advanced Study, July 1947.

8. Third Interim Progress Report on the Physical Realization of an Electronic Computing Instrument, Bigelow, et al. Institute for Advanced Study, January 1948.

9. Fourth Interim Progress Report on the Physical Realization of an Electronic Computing Instrument, Bigelow, et al. Institute for Advanced Study, July 1948.

10. Fifth Interim Progress Report on the Physical Realization of an Electronic Computing Instrument, Bigelow, et al. Institute for Advanced Study, January 1949.

A general reference from which other references may be obtained is: Calculating Instrument and Machines, D. R. Hartree, University of Illinois Press, Urbana, Illinois, 1949.

SUBJECT INDEX

-A-

A Flipflop, 142
A Order, 100, 128, 151
Accumulator, 9, 27, 54
Action, 84
Action Cycle, 78
Action-regenerate Flipflop, 154
Adder, 11, 59
Adder-digit Resolver Test, 232
Adder-digit Resolver Test Block Diagram, 234
Adder-digit Resolver Routine, 236
Adder Voltages, 60
Addition, 11, 125, example of, 22
Address, 26
Address Generator, 57, 83, 159
Address Part of Order, 98
Adjustment of Memory, 90
Amplifier, Video, 82
Analysis of Printout, 196
"And" Circuit, 3
Arithmetic, examples of, 22
Arithmetic Control, 123
Arithmetic Operations, 11
Arithmetic Order, 99
Arithmetic Register, 10, 27, 55, 56
Arithmetic Stop Chassis, 115
Arithmetic Unit, 2, 9, 44, 45
Arithmetic Unit, Malfunctions in, 198
Astigmatism, 91
Asynchronism, 100

-B-

B Flipflop, 142
Balance of Gates, 52
Beam Positioning, 84
Binary Decimal, 7
Binary Numbers, 5
Binary System, 4
Black Clear, 54, 56, 58
Black Gate, 53, 55
Bleeder Chain, 88

273

-C-

-E-

-F-

LIST OF DRAWINGS

INDEX OF DRAWINGS

www.ingramcontent.com/pod-product-compliance
Lightning Source LLC
Chambersburg PA
CBHW071406050326
40689CB00010B/1773